SPECIAL REPORTS

THE
OPIOID CRISIS

BY DUCHESS HARRIS, JD, PHD WITH JOHN L. HAKALA

Essential Library

An Imprint of Abdo Publishing | abdobooks.com

abdobooks.com

Published by Abdo Publishing, a division of ABDO, PO Box 398166, Minneapolis, Minnesota 55439. Copyright © 2019 by Abdo Consulting Group, Inc. International copyrights reserved in all countries. No part of this book may be reproduced in any form without written permission from the publisher. Essential Library™ is a trademark and logo of Abdo Publishing.

Printed in the United States of America, North Mankato, Minnesota
072018
012019

Cover Photo: Victor Moussa/Shutterstock Images
Interior Photos: John Minchillo/AP Images, 4–5; iStockphoto, 8, 19, 26–27, 33, 36–37, 50, 60–61, 96; Red Line Editorial, 10; Cliff Owen/AP Images, 15; Abdul Khaliq/ AP Images, 16–17; Denis D'ttmann/picture-alliance/dpa/AP Images, 25; Diego Cervo/ Shutterstock Images, 41; J. Stone/Shutterstock Images, 46–47; Fang Xia Nuo/ iStockphoto, 48–49; Damir Khabirov/Shutterstock Images, 54; Elaine Thompson/ AP Images, 56; Kyle Mazza/NurPhoto/Sipa USA/AP Images, 59; Drew Angerer/ Getty Images News/Getty Images, 67; Donald Gruener/iStockphoto, 69; Joe Raedel/ Getty Images News/Getty Images, 71; Bernard Well/Toronto Star/Getty Images, 72–73; Kevin D. Liles/AP Images, 77; Paul Harris, CelebrityHomePhotos/Newscom, 81; Shutterstock Images, 82–83; Wave Break Media/Shutterstock Images, 84; STR/ LatinContent WO/Getty Images, 88; Dominic Valente/The Daily Herald/AP Images, 92–93

Editor: Alyssa Krekelberg
Series Designer: Maggie Villaume

Library of Congress Control Number: 2018948307

Publisher's Cataloging-in-Publication Data

Names: Harris, Duchess, author. | Hakala, John L., author.
Title: The opioid crisis / by Duchess Harris and John L. Hakala.
Description: Minneapolis, Minnesota : Abdo Publishing, 2019 | Series: Special
      reports set 4 | Includes online resources and index.
Identifiers: ISBN 9781532116797 (lib. bdg.) | ISBN 9781532159633 (ebook)
Subjects: LCSH: Medication abuse--Juvenile literature. | Opioids--Juvenile
      literature. | Drug abuse--Social aspects--United States--Juvenile literature. |
      Drug abuse--Juvenile literature.
Classification: DDC 362.293--dc23

CONTENTS

CHAPTER ONE

TRAGEDY
STRIKES

An entire community was devastated on May 26, 2017. There was no hurricane, tornado, or wildfire to blame. The culprits were two syringes filled with opioids. Eighteen-year-old Joseph Abraham and 19-year-old Dustin Manning were both found dead in Lawrenceville, Georgia. They were childhood friends just beginning their adult lives. Although they had not been in contact with each other for several years, both lost their lives to opioid overdoses on the same day, just one-half mile (0.8 km) apart.[1]

The two young men had incredible potential, but it was overshadowed by personal problems that led to drug use. Manning began feeling the effects of depression at age 12 and soon turned to drugs,

First responders are getting more calls related to overdoses as the opioid crisis continues.

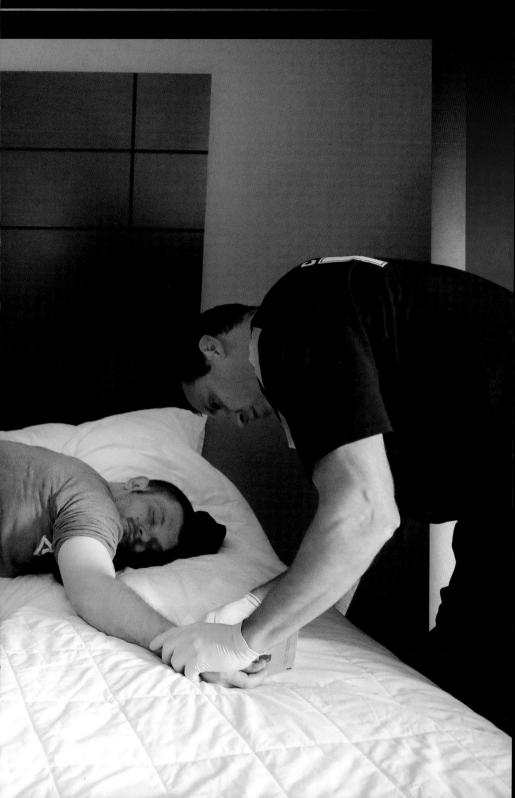

hoping to find relief. He always had ambitions of joining the military. Abraham was an avid fisherman who loved spending time outdoors. When he was in eighth grade, two of his close friends died and Abraham began using drugs as a way to cope. For both Manning and Abraham, drug abuse led to the opioid addictions that caused their deaths.

Toxicology reports indicated the drugs that caused the men to overdose were a lethal combination of heroin and fentanyl. Combining heroin and fentanyl is particularly deadly. Drug dealers sometimes add dangerous amounts of fentanyl to heroin to boost the drug's potency. Heroin is an illegal street drug, whereas fentanyl is a powerful lab-created pain reliever, routinely prescribed for medical conditions. Both belong to the classification of drugs known as opioids. According to the National Institute on Drug Abuse (NIDA), opioids cause euphoria and relief from physical pain. These effects are what lead many people to develop opioid addictions.

Police reports indicated the drugs that Manning and Abraham used were supplied in nearly identical wrappings. This led police to speculate that the drugs were purchased from the same dealer. Authorities believe they knew who supplied the drugs, but they lacked sufficient evidence to make an arrest. The community was horrified by the possibility of others getting their hands on the same deadly opioids. Considering how closely together the deaths occurred, neighbors were concerned that another tragedy was right around the corner.

Manning's and Abraham's parents are involved in a support group that helps people cope with the loss of children to opioid overdoses. The support group is a reflection of societal trends. The Mannings and Abrahams are just two of the many families

DEADLIER THAN WAR

War often brings a large number of injuries and deaths. For the United States, the Vietnam War (1954–1975) was no exception. Approximately 58,000 people serving in the US military died during this conflict. That is an average of roughly 2,800 casualties per year.[3]

Although many people view this conflict as especially deadly, it is nowhere near as lethal as the opioid crisis. In 2016, more than 64,000 people died of drug overdoses, and the majority of overdoses were caused by opioids.[4] While the opioid crisis may not provide the same level of violence as war, the crisis has proven to be more lethal than many armed conflicts. Perhaps the deadliest battle the United States has ever engaged in is being fought within local communities and hospitals.

trying to cope with this type of tragedy. The group sees a steady increase in participants, which mirrors the national pattern of opioid overdoses. The parents of Abraham and Manning are reminded every day of the effects of opioids. "You change. You're never going [to] be the same. I'll never be the person I was. It's like a knife deep in your heart," said Manning's mother, Lisa.[5] The opioid issue has become far more than a problem. It is now a full-blown crisis.

WHAT IS THE OPIOID CRISIS?

Opioid drugs are highly effective painkillers. The drugs' namesake, opium, is produced by the poppy plant, which humans have cultivated for centuries. The plant is used in many forms, which are called derivatives. Common derivatives of opium are morphine, codeine, oxycodone, and heroin. Each of these derivatives was

Oxycodone has a high risk for abuse and addiction.

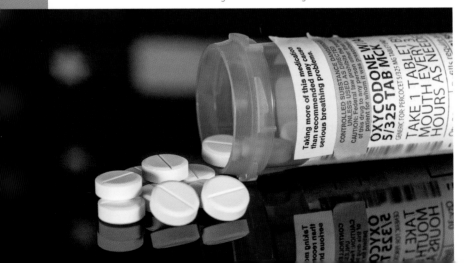

once used for medicinal purposes. Morphine, codeine, and oxycodone are still routinely prescribed by hospitals and clinics. Fentanyl is a commonly prescribed synthetic opioid. It is not a derivative of the poppy plant, and it produces stronger effects than natural opioids. Fentanyl is laboratory created and is 50 to 100 times more potent than morphine.[6]

Because opioids are so effective at reducing pain, health-care providers began to prescribe these drugs at an ever-increasing rate. In the late 1990s, pharmaceutical companies assured medical professionals that their patients would not become addicted to opioids. The experts turned out to be wrong—opioids were found to be highly addictive. This failed promise, combined with the drugs' effectiveness, led to an explosion of opioid use, misuse, and addiction. Doctors today are placed in a difficult position. They struggle with striking a balance between effective treatments and possible damages to their patients.

This widespread opioid consumption has led to alarming addiction statistics. According to NIDA, between 21 and 29 percent of all patients prescribed opioids

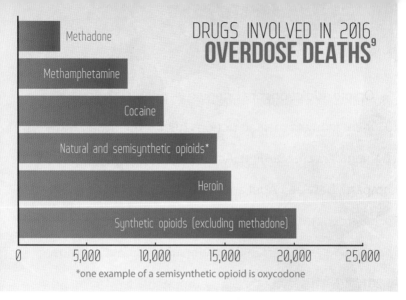

DRUGS INVOLVED IN 2016 OVERDOSE DEATHS[9]

- Methadone
- Methamphetamine
- Cocaine
- Natural and semisynthetic opioids*
- Heroin
- Synthetic opioids (excluding methadone)

0   5,000   10,000   15,000   20,000   25,000

*one example of a semisynthetic opioid is oxycodone

More than 64,000 people died from drug overdoses in 2016, and a large portion of them involved opioids.

for chronic pain misuse them. Of this population, 8 to 12 percent develop an opioid use disorder. It is estimated that nearly two million people in the United States suffer from this type of disorder. Between 4 and 6 percent of those who abuse prescription opioids make the dangerous transition to heroin. Approximately 80 percent of heroin users first abused prescribed opioid painkillers.[7] Mike Vigil, the former chief of internal operations at the Drug Enforcement Administration (DEA), explains why people switch from using prescription opioids to heroin: "The big moneymaker right now, given the opioid epidemic, is heroin, and the reason that it's heroin is that people who have become addicted to prescription opioids find it a lot cheaper to purchase heroin."[8]

Opioid addictions are bringing people straight back to where many of their addictions began: the hospital. The numbers are startling. According to OM1, a data company, between April and June of 2017, nearly one of six emergency room visits was related to opioids.[10] More than 35,000 Americans died as a result of opioid overdose in 2016.[11] Trends show that this number is likely to increase with time. An opioid overdose occurs when a person takes a dose of an opioid that is too strong, causing the person's breathing to slow or stop.

The United States is in the middle of an opioid epidemic. The effects of opioid abuse are being experienced throughout many communities. Massachusetts senator Ed Markey warns, "The terrorist threat families in America see is not in the streets of Aleppo [in Syria]. It's fentanyl coming down your street."[12]

THE MANY FACES OF THE CRISIS

The effects of the opioid crisis are devastating on many levels. Individual lives are destroyed by substance abuse. Families are torn apart by addiction and by the deaths of loved ones. Cities and towns are struggling to keep up with increased medical events and criminal activity. The effects add up to a nation overburdened by a drug-induced dilemma. On some level, many US citizens find their lives affected by the consequences of the opioid epidemic. In addition, numerous industries are strained by the crisis.

This epidemic affects all types of individuals struggling with physical or psychological pain. Celebrities are no exception. Many actors and musicians have died from opioid overdoses. Heath Ledger, Philip Seymour Hoffman, Prince, and Tom Petty are just a few examples of performers whose deaths were attributed to overdoses of opioid painkillers mixed with other drugs. Legendary music icon Elvis Presley also battled with an addiction to painkillers prior to his death in 1977. Unfortunately, overdose deaths are becoming a nearly routine occurrence. Andrew Kolodny, an addiction expert at Brandeis University, says, "No one is surprised when they hear about a rock star dying of a drug overdose."[13]

With opioids causing so much damage on a national and global scale, it is important for researchers and addiction experts to dig to the roots of the problem. Only then can ideas for practical solutions be discovered. It is going to take a large network to solve the opioid crisis. Experts believe families, medical professionals, law enforcement personnel, politicians, and many others need to come together to develop solutions before the crisis spins out of control. The first place to look is at the drugs themselves. It is critical to understand exactly where these substances come from.

A STAR'S STORY

Ben Haggerty, known by his stage name Macklemore, is an American singer, rapper, and activist. Although many people are familiar with his music, some do not know of his personal struggles with opioid addiction. "I couldn't get away from the shadow that opioids had cast over my life. My love for making music was gone," the singer confessed.[14]

Beginning as a teenager, he struggled with addictions that started with alcohol and evolved to an opioid medication called OxyContin. Besides the damage to his music-making, many of his personal relationships were destroyed. At age 25 he sought rehab services, which helped him personally and professionally heal. His philosophy is that society needs to focus on treatment solutions rather than punishing drug abusers. Macklemore believes compassion is the best path to recovery.

FROM THE
HEADLINES

MASSIVE NEW JERSEY DRUG BUST

In 2017, two men were arrested for possessing and planning to sell a dangerous material. The substance, if distributed, had the potential to harm as many people as the entire population of New Jersey and New York City combined. It wasn't a nuclear bomb or biological weapon, but rather 100 pounds (45 kg) of the drug fentanyl. Many lives were potentially saved by this drug seizure.

"Because dealers use this super-potent opioid to boost heroin and create counterfeit oxy pills, drug users are left to play a deadly game of Russian roulette each time they give way to their addiction," said New Jersey attorney general Gurbir Grewal. In New Jersey, there were more than 800 fentanyl-related deaths in 2016, nearly double the previous year's total. Director of the New Jersey Division of Criminal Justice Elie Honig notes that nearly one-third of tested heroin in New Jersey contains fentanyl.

The two suspects, Jesus Carrillo-Pineda of Philadelphia and Daniel Vasquez of Arizona, pleaded guilty and faced ten and six years in prison, respectively. Had their scheme not been discovered, they would have supplied nearly 18 million doses of fentanyl into the black market.[15]

Fentanyl can be made into a liquid, tablet, or powder form.

CHAPTER TWO

THE HISTORY
OF OPIOIDS

The poppy plant and its many opioid products were used long before they sparked a crisis in the United States. Early civilizations, developing countries, and world powers all found ways to harness the power of this plant. From ancient trading routes to modern interstate highways, the poppy plant has crossed many empires.

WORLD HISTORY

The earliest record of the poppy plant being routinely utilized by humans dates back to 3400 BCE, by the Sumerian people in Mesopotamia. They referred to the poppy as *hul gil*, or the "joy plant." This plant quickly

The pod of the poppy plant can be sliced open to get the most basic form of opium.

became a sought-after crop and spread throughout the Middle East.

Knowledge of poppy cultivation moved throughout the region. In addition, during the 1300s BCE, the Egyptians grew large fields of poppies. The thick, syrupy raw opium sap from the poppy plant creates a potent chewable drug. This drug was used by ancient societies as a sleeping and pain-relieving medication. Evidence also shows that opium was used as a numbing medication for surgeries. The opium trade was highly successful by the time of King Tutankhamen, who is thought to have lived between 1343 and 1323 BCE. The powerful Egyptian empire moved the highly profitable opium product to cities along the Mediterranean Sea. Nearly ten centuries later, during his 300 BCE travels, Greek conqueror Alexander the Great brought opium to India and Persia.

The two kingdoms of India and Persia were critical gateways along the famous Silk Road. The Silk Road was an extensive trading network used from around 130 BCE to the mid-1400s CE that connected Europe to India and China and the many other nations between them. It was a vital link between the Eastern and the Western worlds.

The Silk Road created a market for the purchase and transportation of many goods, including opium. Opium is believed to have been first introduced to China through the Silk Road in 500 or 600 CE.

The Silk Road became obsolete once large sailing ships were able to navigate between the West and the East. These vessels made long-distance trade easier. Thanks to their growing naval supremacy, the British became the leaders in global trade in the 1600s. In 1699, the British East India Company began trading with the Chinese. The British bought tea, silk, and porcelain from China in exchange for silver. As tea became very popular in England, the British feared they were losing too much silver. The East India Company grew opium in the British-controlled region of

The British East India Company was formed in 1600.

India. This opium was then transported by ship and sold to China in place of silver. The drug began to enter China in massive quantities.

Throughout the following decades, addictions became commonplace in China. This problem led Emperor Yongzheng to ban the domestic sale and smoking of opium except for licensed medical purposes in 1729. Despite this ban, the problem continued to grow, and opium products became completely illegal to grow, trade, or use in 1796 under Emperor Jiaqing. This did not stop the British from bringing the drug to Chinese shores.

The British East India Company had monopolized opium trading by 1800. Soon, the British began to transport opium throughout the world, including to the United States. The British continued to smuggle the illegal drug into

BRITISH EAST INDIA COMPANY

The British East India Company was a vital supply line allowing trade between England, East Asia, and India. The East India Company is credited with bringing together some Eastern and Western cultural influences. While initially only concerned with the business of trading goods and silver, the company eventually moved on to become involved in political and controversial trade industries across the world, including slavery and the smuggling of opium into China. This illegal smuggling led to armed conflicts called the Opium Wars. The company began losing significant political power by the mid-1800s and officially ceased as an organization in 1873.

China, which greatly upset the Chinese leadership. This led to two armed conflicts that pitted the East against the West. The conflicts were known as the Opium Wars. The first Opium War occurred between 1839 and 1842. The second Opium War lasted from 1856 to 1860. Determined to expand the opium trade in China, the British successfully defeated Chinese forces in both events, although the French aided the British in the second Opium War. These results ultimately led to several new ports opening in China. Consequently, the import of opium to China was once again legalized in 1858. This led to an increase in both British profits and Chinese addiction rates.

A NEW CENTURY, A NEW VISION

It is thought that opium has been in the United States since the *Mayflower* landed in 1620. Pilgrim physician Samuel Fuller was believed to have carried an opium-based medication in his medical kit. During the American Revolution (1775–1783), opium was commonly used in a medicine called laudanum.

By 1900, many Americans had developed an addiction to opioids or were dependent on them. President

Theodore Roosevelt viewed this as more than a problem. He believed it was a crisis that threatened the strength of the nation. In 1908, he appointed an Ohio physician, Hamilton Wright, to become the first opioid commissioner.

In 1909, opium importation was prohibited in the United States. The following year, China was able to convince the British to dismantle their India-China opium trade. Wright believed this was great news. He helped create the Harrison Narcotics Act, which passed on December 17, 1914. This law required all pharmacists, doctors, and manufacturers to pay a tax and join a national registry to prescribe these drugs. Anyone who was caught with unregistered drugs faced heavy fines and prison time. The goal was to limit drug use to legitimate medical purposes. However, this was deemed by the US government to be not enough. Narcotic drugs such as heroin and cocaine were prohibited in the mid-1920s, beginning about the same time as alcohol prohibition.

The ban on drugs did not stop the influx and usage of opioids in the United States.

"IT [OPIUM] HAS ROBBED TEN THOUSAND BUSINESSMEN OF MORAL SENSE AND MADE THEM BEASTS WHO PREY UPON THEIR FELLOWS."[1]

—HAMILTON WRIGHT, 1911

Individuals looking for the drugs turned to the black market, and heroin was one opioid drug people bought. It was first created in England in the late 1800s by the Bayer Pharmaceutical Company. It was soon being illegally produced all over the world.

Chinese heroin became a common illegal commodity in the United States during the 1930s. New York City became a hotbed for heroin distribution and use. In response to growing concerns, President Richard Nixon created the DEA on July 1, 1973. Today, this federal organization continues to take on the nation's drug issues.

During the mid-1970s, the heroin epidemic cooled down. However, this was not because of a lack of interest in the drugs. The decline was due to a reduction in the supply of heroin's ingredients. The Vietnam War (1954–1975) disrupted the supply of raw opium from Southeast Asia. Illegal suppliers and users needed a new source, and they found it in Mexico.

RECENT HISTORY

In the 2000s, several economically challenged countries turned to the heroin and opioid trade as a source of revenue. Afghanistan produces 95 percent of the world's raw opium.[2] This opium is responsible for nearly all the heroin consumed in Europe, Africa, the Middle East, large areas of Canada, and the Pacific nations.

Mexico has once again become a powerful producer of poppies. As American demand for opioids increased in the 2000s, so did Mexico's supply of poppies. In 2016, Mexico grew enough poppy plants to produce around 178,000 pounds (81,000 kg) of heroin.[3] In 2017, the DEA reported that Mexico was the largest supplier of illegal opioids and heroin to the United States, largely due to the two countries' close proximity.

Although many headlines during the late 1990s and early 2000s focused on illegal drugs such as heroin, physicians were increasing the number of prescriptions for legal opioid medications. From 1996 to 2001, the pharmaceutical company Purdue Pharma aggressively marketed medicinal opioids, especially OxyContin. The company spent hundreds of millions of dollars on promotional materials and seminars to convince physicians to prescribe these products to patients. Purdue even gave patients coupons for a free seven- to 30-day supply. That

In 2017, Mexican forces found and destroyed some illegal poppy fields.

program ended in 2001, but not before tens of thousands of coupons were used.

During its promotional push, Purdue touted OxyContin as having an extremely small risk for addiction. Salespeople were instructed to report the risk as less than 1 percent. This was later determined to be wildly misleading. In 2007, the drug company pleaded guilty to making false claims about its product and was forced to pay $634 million in fines.[4] However, the damage caused by the increase in prescribed opioids was far more costly. Many people wonder how this family of drugs has taken over the lives of so many. The answers lie in the science and chemistry sealed within the drugs.

CHAPTER THREE

THE SCIENCE
OF THE CRISIS

O pioids have demonstrated their effectiveness and dangers throughout history. Countless people have become addicted to these drugs. To understand how the crisis has exploded into what it is today, it is critical to understand how the drugs work and how they cause harm.

FROM PLANTS TO DRUGS

Most species of poppy plants do not contain substances that can be used to make drugs. Many poppies are purchased for decorative purposes. Other harmless poppies are found growing in the wild. Only the opium poppy (*Papaver somniferum*) contains opium. This plant can be found in many areas of the world today.

The reward pathway plays a role in addiction. The pathway is found in the brain's frontal lobe.

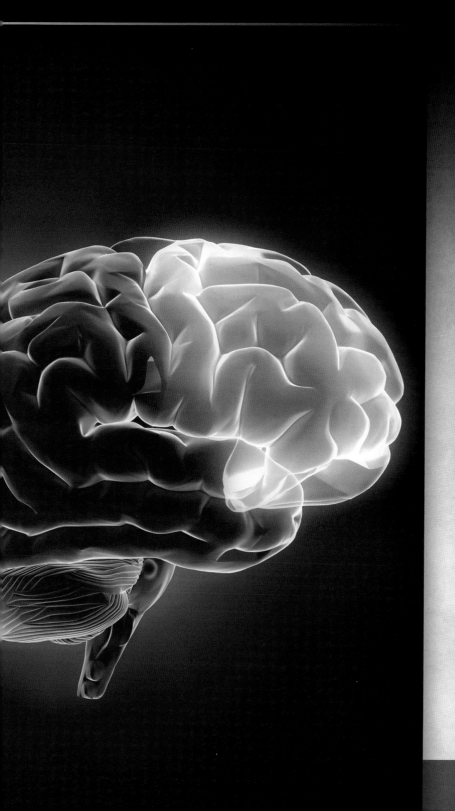

Also called the white poppy, this plant typically grows three to 16 feet (0.9 to 4.9 m) in height, with various colors of flowers. The part of the plant used for medicinal and illicit purposes is the sap. This milky sap, called latex, comes from the unripe seed head of the plant. The latex contains chemical compounds that are found in opium, morphine, and codeine. The latex is opium in its most basic form. The opium poppy also produces harmless seeds and oils. The oils are commonly used for baking.

The latex is extracted from the plant by cutting the seed pod vertically in parallel strokes. The sap slowly begins to spill out. As this happens, it becomes darker and thicker. The end result is a dark brown or black sticky gumlike substance. The poppy farmer then scrapes the latex off the plant, forms it into bundles, and wraps this drug in leaves or plastic.

AN ACCIDENTAL DISCOVERY

English researcher Charles Romley Alder Wright discovered a powerful new medication in 1874. This was done by mixing morphine with other chemicals. He quickly discontinued his research after the medication caused him anxiety, sleepiness, and vomiting after he administered it to himself. The drug company Bayer picked up on his research and promoted the medication's effectiveness for treating respiratory problems. It was quickly made available over the counter. However, this drug didn't stay on the shelves for too long. This new drug, called heroin, caused more problems than it solved.

To obtain stronger varieties of opioids, this latex goes through a chemical altering process called refining. Opium is easily refined into a more powerful and transportation-ready form. In a process that involves boiling, filtering, and chemical separation, the opium becomes a brown paste that is poured into molds. Once it is dried in the sun, the product is called morphine base. This product is now ready to process into medical products. It can also be converted into heroin. Changing morphine base into other drugs requires specialized lab techniques and equipment.

OPIOIDS AND THE BRAIN

The brain is a complex organ made of nerve cells called neurons. These interconnected neurons are extremely efficient at sending and receiving messages within the brain and throughout the rest of the body. The part of the neuron that sends messages is called the axon. The receiving centers on neurons are called dendrites. When the axon of one neuron meets dendrites of another, they create a gap known as a synapse. This tiny gap is where one neuron sends messages to the next.

Signals between neurons are carried by chemical messengers called neurotransmitters. Neurotransmitters are accepted on dendrites by structures called receptors. This process repeats from neuron to neuron until the original signal reaches its destination. This rapid transfer of neurotransmitters between neurons allows humans to move, think, feel, and communicate.

When opioids enter the body, they travel to the brain. Once in the brain, opioids flood specific opioid-receptor sites. The brain already has opioid-binding sites because the body is able to naturally produce pain-reducing opioids. However, the body is not capable of producing enough opioids to block pain or create an overdose. The drugs trick the brain into thinking the drugs are natural.

> "ALL OPIOIDS ARE CHEMICALLY RELATED AND INTERACT WITH OPIOID RECEPTORS ON NERVE CELLS IN THE BODY AND BRAIN."[1]
>
> —NIDA

Once the nerve cells recognize that the opioid receptors are filled, neurons release the powerful neurotransmitter called dopamine. Dopamine creates strong sensations of reward and pleasure. Excess dopamine causes overstimulation of the brain. This leads to a state of extreme excitement or happiness called euphoria. The brain enjoys this state of mind and remembers exactly what it took to get the feeling. This mechanism is the brain's natural tool to encourage learning new behaviors. While some pleasurable behaviors are good, other repeated behaviors cause serious problems.

If this reward system is repeatedly triggered by drugs, it creates a chemical dependency problem. This condition is also known as a drug addiction.

When opioids are used, dopamine is released and the body feels good. When opioids are not present, the body feels as though something is missing. After long-term opioid abuse, the brain will gradually stop producing its own dopamine. With the absence of dopamine, the brain craves more opioids and sends powerful messages

GENETIC FACTORS

A 2017 study in the journal *Biological Psychiatry* suggests there are genetic factors that lead to opioid addiction. The study analyzed Americans of European and African descent who were exposed to opioids, some of whom were addicted to opioids.

The research indicates the subjects who demonstrated opioid addiction often had a variation near a gene called RGMA. While the exact method is still unknown, this gene variation causes an increase of signals to the front of the brain called the frontal lobe. This region of the brain is responsible for decision-making. This change in brain signaling, and decision-making, is important in understanding opioid dependency. This information has potential to someday help doctors properly prescribe or restrict opioids with patients who are more likely to become addicted.

signaling its need for more of the drug. The easiest way to fill this need is for a person to take more opioids. This creates a vicious cycle that some people find very hard to break.

Since the brain reacts to all types of opioids the same way, people with addictions seek any type of opioid available. Prescription medications and heroin fill this void. As a person's addiction grows stronger, more powerful versions of opioids or combinations of various drugs are required to get the same feel-good effect. This leads to drug use and abuse.

"AS YOU REDUCE THE SUPPLY OF PRESCRIPTION DRUGS, ADDICTS AREN'T GOING TO STOP USING."[2]

—THEODORE CICERO, PROFESSOR OF PSYCHIATRY, WASHINGTON UNIVERSITY SCHOOL OF MEDICINE

HOW OPIOIDS ARE USED

Researchers and individuals have discovered different ways to introduce opioids into the body. Each leads to different effects. Eating opium products is the most common and historical method of consuming these drugs. Earliest records of opium use show ancient people

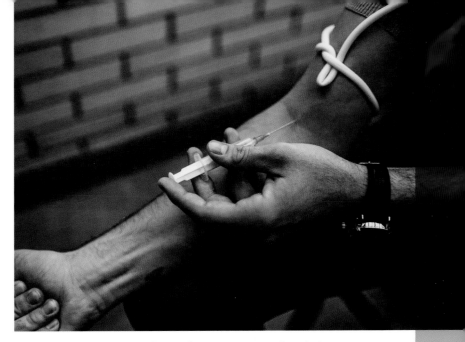

Injecting opioids into veins brings the fastest sense of euphoria to users.

chewing the plant. The practice of chewing opium plants and latex is still practiced today. In the United States, opioid medications are commonly found in pill form. Once the pills are swallowed, they are broken down by the digestive system and absorbed into the bloodstream. When the drugs reach the brain, they produce euphoria.

In the 1800s, smoking opium was a common method of using the poppy plant. It was the principle activity in opium dens. This method of consuming opioids is called inhalation. Breathing in the smoke and vapors of opium introduces the drug into the lungs. The lungs filter air in and out of the body through structures called alveoli. The drug passes through the alveoli and enters the

MORE TO THE
STORY

DIFFERENT NEUROTRANSMITTERS

Dopamine is not the only important neurotransmitter in the human body. Five other critical chemical messengers are acetylcholine, norepinephrine, GABA, glutamate, and serotonin.

Acetylcholine is responsible for stimulating muscles. Without this neurotransmitter, muscles do not move or function. Norepinephrine prepares the body for dangerous or stressful situations. It raises heart rate and blood pressure. It also plays an important role in forming and storing memories. GABA is essentially the braking system for the brain, as it blocks neurons from firing. It helps slow down neurotransmitters that excite the mind. Glutamate is the most common neurotransmitter in the brain. It excites the brain and is also important for memory. Serotonin, like dopamine, affects emotion and mood. Depression is caused by too little serotonin. While opioids don't directly act on these other five neurotransmitters, altering the brain's chemical makeup with opioids has the potential to indirectly and dangerously shift the balance of neurotransmitters.

bloodstream. Inhalation is a more direct path to the brain because the drug avoids being filtered out by the liver. The drug's effect is weakened if the drug passes through the liver before getting to the brain.

The most direct pathway to the brain is by direct injection into the bloodstream. It is also extremely dangerous if not done by a medical professional. Heroin is most commonly used through this method. The user melts down solid heroin, draws it into a medical syringe, and injects it into a vein with a needle. Other opioid medications, such as fentanyl, are often crushed and added to the syringe. This directly puts all the opioid substances into the bloodstream, yielding the fastest and strongest reaction. The body has no defense mechanism it can use against the injected flood of drugs. Quite often, this technique leads to an overdose and death. Death can occur within a matter of hours, minutes, or even seconds.

CHAPTER FOUR

THE EFFECTS ON
INDIVIDUALS

O pioid abuse and addictions can cause lasting effects on individuals. Major damage can occur to an addicted person's health and relationships with others. These changes are not just short-term consequences. They have the ability to change the course of a person's entire life.

PHYSICAL AND MENTAL DAMAGE

Once opioids are introduced into the body, a person experiences the initial surge of dopamine euphoria. During this time, the user feels a warm flushing sensation in the skin, a dry mouth, and heaviness in the arms and legs. Immediate side effects also include nausea, vomiting, and itchiness.

People with addictions might rearrange their whole lives to revolve around a substance.

After the initial rush wears off, it's common for users to feel drowsy, with clouded mental functions, a decreased heart rate, and slowed breathing. Breathing stops if a user takes too strong a dose. This leads to unconsciousness, coma, possible brain damage, and, in many cases, an overdose death. As Dr. Karen Drexler, from Emory University, explains, "Usually when you are sleeping, your body naturally remembers to breathe. In the case of a heroin overdose, you fall asleep and essentially your body forgets."[1]

The long-term effects of opioid abuse are harsh. Users develop a tolerance as they increase their quantity and frequency of opioid use. Tolerance for a drug will force a person to use more and more of the substance to feel the same effects. Therefore,

CLASSIFYING DRUGS

There are many types of drugs. The drugs fall into certain categories called classes. The three most commonly abused classes of prescription drugs are opioids, depressants, and stimulants.

Opioids are painkillers that cause a sense of euphoria. Depressants are used to slow down brain activity. Depressant drugs are used for sleeping and antianxiety medications. Commonly prescribed stimulants include Adderall and Ritalin. Like opioids, stimulants can also cause euphoria. Stimulants also cause an increase in heart rate and blood pressure. One example of a stimulant drug is cocaine. Misuse of stimulants can lead to dangerously high body temperature, fatal cardiovascular failure, and seizures.

tolerance leads to an urge for more frequent drug use and stronger opioids.

Users will experience withdrawal if they don't get the drugs their bodies are addicted to. Withdrawal is a series of physical conditions caused by the lack of a drug. Symptoms of short-term opioid withdrawal include muscular pain, restlessness, vomiting, diarrhea, cold flashes, and uncontrolled movement.

The first wave of short-term withdrawal is just the beginning of a person's recovery from addiction. Recovery that lasts months or years is called post–acute withdrawal syndrome. During this time, the recovering person feels tired and lacks motivation. The individual is also much more sensitive to minor sources of pain. These symptoms are caused by opioid-induced changes to the brain. Due to the expectation of new opioids, the brain decreases production of painkilling hormones called endorphins. There is also an increase in the number of opioid receptors after long-term abuse. An increase in opioid

"IN ALL MY YEARS AS A PHYSICIAN, I HAVE NEVER, EVER MET AN ADDICTED PERSON WHO WANTED TO BE AN ADDICT."[2]

—DR. NORA VOLKOW, NIDA DIRECTOR

receptors in the brain leads to increased frequency and strength of opioid cravings. This combination leads to a miserable road to recovery for some people.

LONG-TERM CONSEQUENCES

Ongoing health effects of opioid abuse go beyond the brain. There is a risk that the heart's lining and valves will become infected. Infection often leads to heart failure if left untreated. Heart failure is a condition in which the heart does not efficiently pump blood to the rest of the body. Significant heart failure requires surgery and is commonly fatal if left untreated.

Other vital organs are also affected by opioid abuse. Long-term depressed breathing from opioids leads to lung diseases such as pneumonia. Pneumonia is a potentially deadly inflammation of the lungs caused by infection. The lung's alveoli fill with fluid, which makes breathing difficult or impossible. The kidneys also receive damage from opioid abuse, which is sometimes permanent. Recovery

from kidney failure includes dialysis and a possible organ transplant.

Unsafe injection practices lead to extreme health consequences. One of the deadliest long-term risks is contracting HIV/AIDS. HIV/AIDS is commonly spread between heroin users who share hypodermic needles. More than one million people in the United States have HIV. Nearly 10 percent of these individuals do not know they have the condition.[4]

Mental health is also affected by abusing opioids. Studies show that opioid use causes or worsens mood and anxiety disorders in users. Examples of these ailments include depression, bipolar disorder, and anxiety disorders. Researchers estimate 48 percent of people addicted to heroin experience depression. Heroin users have a

THE YOUNGEST VICTIMS

Opioid abuse is not only dangerous to the health of the user. If a pregnant woman uses prescription opioids or heroin, there are serious consequences for her child. One potential problem is neonatal abstinence syndrome (NAS). NAS is on the rise in the United States.

NAS occurs when newborn babies withdraw from drugs that their mothers were using during pregnancy. The drugs cross into the fetus through the umbilical cord. The umbilical cord is the vital line fetuses use to receive food and oxygen. Symptoms of this disease in newborns include shaking, breathing problems, slow weight gain, and trouble sleeping. If not treated properly, the baby experiences critical health problems. This condition sometimes results in death.

suicide rate of 35 percent.[5] In addition to the physical and mental consequences, families and friendships are frequently affected by drug abuse.

DESTROYING RELATIONSHIPS

Alex Gurvis was a military police officer for the Army National Guard. In 2005, he sustained an injury while on active duty. He was prescribed OxyContin for his pain. By 2008, Gurvis had developed an addiction to opioids, and his addiction became bad enough that his wife convinced him to go to rehab. His time in rehab lasted only a couple of days because Gurvis was convinced he didn't have a problem.

His addiction began to spin out of control. Throughout the following decade, Gurvis experienced relationship problems, was involved in several car accidents, and was constantly in and out of court. He even stole his mother's $10,000 wedding ring to buy drugs.[6] In 2013, Gurvis's doctor lost his medical license for overprescribing pain medication. Similar to so many people addicted to opioids, Gurvis needed stronger drugs to feel the same level of euphoric effects. Eventually he turned to heroin.

On January 1, 2017, Gurvis died of an opioid overdose. He left behind a wife, daughter, and mother. Two days before Gurvis died, his mother asked why he wasn't able to simply throw the pills away. Gurvis said, "I can't live without them, Mom."[7] That was the last time his mother saw him alive.

Gurvis's story is far from unique. Many opioid abusers begin with a simple prescription for a legitimate medical purpose. Once the prescription runs out, it is not necessarily the end of their opioid use. Opioid abusers act in ways they normally wouldn't as the brain's dependency and the user's financial burden worsens. Ultimately the strain becomes so strong that it tears some families apart. Until his death, Gurvis still had the support of his loved ones. Many are not so lucky, and they face the struggle alone.

TOGETHER, ALONE

Hundreds of thousands of people are homeless in the United States. Many factors are responsible for this statistic, but opioid addictions are a large contributor. As a person's addiction grows stronger, the habit becomes more expensive. The costs become so great that some people can no longer afford their homes. Any source of money is typically used to feed the addiction. This pushes many drug abusers out onto the street.

In the 2016 Annual Homelessness Assessment Report, nearly one of five people who were homeless had a chronic substance abuse disorder.[8] The report does not distinguish between those who became addicted before becoming homeless or after. Between 2003 and 2008, approximately 28,000 people

SUCCESS STORY

Cortney Lovell's drug addiction caused her to resort to desperate measures that betrayed her personal morals and beliefs. Lovell is a former heroin user who is in long-term recovery. During the height of her addiction, she stole money from many people and businesses. She had numerous criminal charges, including dozens of felonies, by age 19. Lovell was desperate to get more drugs, but she finally gave up. She decided to take a dose of heroin mixed with cocaine. She assumed it would kill her, but it didn't. After spending time in jail and years in therapy, Lovell now works as a public speaker, addiction counselor, and recovery coach in her hometown of North Chatham, New York.

who were homeless in the Boston, Massachusetts, area died. Nearly 17 percent of these deaths were from drug overdoses. Of that group, 81 percent of the drug overdoses involved opioids.[9] In 2013, a report indicated that drug overdoses had become the top killer of homeless people.

The cost of the opioid crisis is huge. Tremendous financial burdens are placed on individuals. This cost begins to spread to the community. Medical costs, treatment expenses, and lost wages are draining the nation. While the most tragic examples of opioid loss come from individual struggles, society is suffering as well. Understanding how opioids are affecting society is critical to finding answers for the epidemic.

FROM THE
HEADLINES

LOSING A LEGEND

The famous musician Tom Petty died on October 2, 2017. According to autopsy reports, Petty had four types of opioids in his system: fentanyl, oxycodone, acetyl fentanyl, and despropionyl fentanyl. He had also taken these drugs with powerful sleep medications and an antidepressant.

By all accounts, these drugs were not being used for recreation or enjoyment but to continue performing. He was suffering from a painful hip injury, which was officially diagnosed as a fracture on the day he died. A family statement reads, "Despite this painful injury he insisted on keeping his commitment to his fans and he toured 53 dates with a broken hip and, as he did, it worsened to a more serious injury."[10]

Petty had struggled with heroin addiction in 1997. This followed a divorce from his first wife, Jane Benyo. Petty described this relationship as abusive and a key contributor for his descent into heroin addiction. In 2001, Petty married Dana York but still struggled with addiction in secret before seeking treatment. Petty credited York with saving him and reconnecting him to his children. Unfortunately, opioids would return to his life and result in his death.

Officials believe Tom Petty died from an accidental overdose.

CHAPTER FIVE

SOCIAL
COSTS

T he health-care system plays an important role in the opioid crisis. The amount of prescription opioids sold to hospitals, clinics, and pharmacies quadrupled from 1999 to 2010. During this time, there was no change in the amount of pain patients reported in the United States. Americans were not statistically feeling any increase in the frequency of pain, but the rates of prescribing these powerful painkillers increased rapidly.

In part because of the access to opioids, hospitals throughout the country began to experience an alarming number of patient visits due to opioid abuse. Between 2005 and 2014, the United States saw a 99.4 percent increase in opioid-related emergency

Hospitals experience the burden of the opioid crisis as people suffer from overdoses.

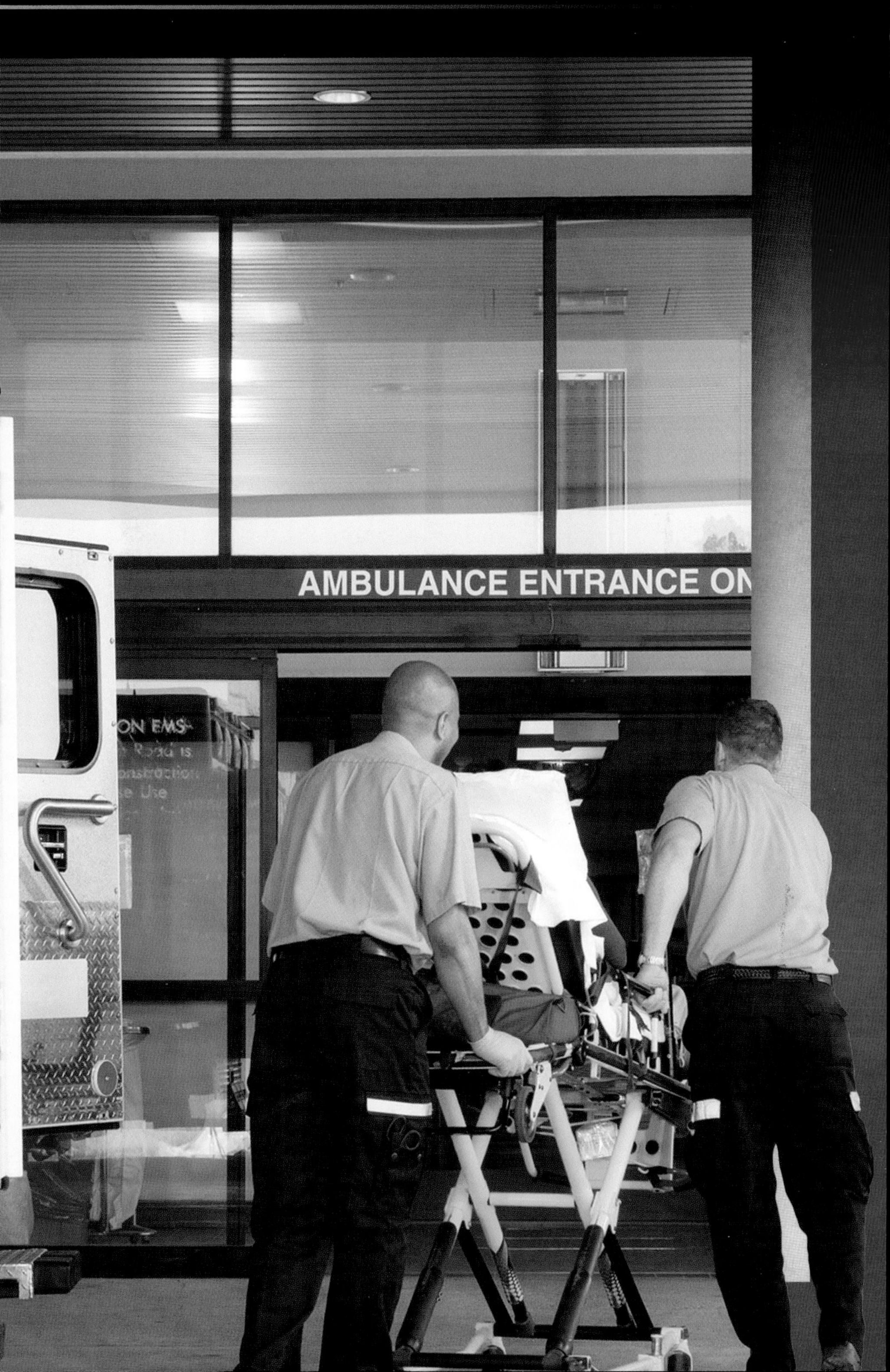
AMBULANCE ENTRANCE ON
ON EMS

room visits. The number of patients requiring multiple-day inpatient hospital treatment rose 64.1 percent.[1] During that same time frame, mental health/substance abuse was the only category that saw an increase in inpatient stays. Categories such as injury, surgical, medical, maternal, and neonatal hospitalizations all saw decreases.

Hospitals also saw an increase in patients who overdosed. Overdoses are especially frightening and are difficult cases to manage. When doctors treat overdose patients, they are often worried about the type of drugs a patient used, the unknown quantities of the drugs, and their overall lack of information about their patients. Even

People of all ages can suffer from opioid addictions.

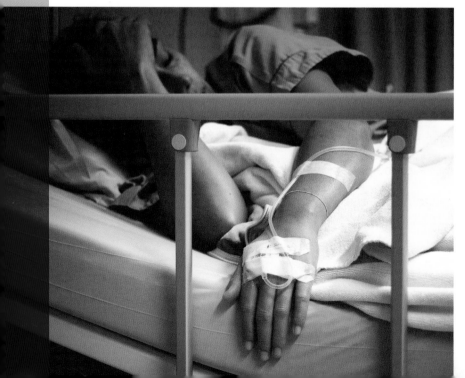

if they are told exactly what was taken, these cases are challenging. Overdoses require specific treatment based on the types and quantities of drugs abused. A patient can die if the wrong type or amount of medication is given.

OVERPRESCRIBING OPIOIDS

Opioids can lead to a variety of medical problems. Despite the risks, many doctors prescribe opioids as the first method of pain defense. A nurse in San Francisco, California, named Dolores Flanagan recounted her experience as a patient. She states, "I recently broke a bone and both in the E.R. and in the M.D. office, was offered opioids as a first-line pain medication. I declined, aware that alternating acetaminophen and ibuprofen, and icing and elevating were better, evidence-based options for acute pain like a broken bone."[2] Had Flanagan not known this information, she might have accepted the opioid drugs. Although opioids are effective pain blockers, there are financial reasons why some doctors have been quick to prescribe opioids.

"DESPITE THE EXTRA DISCOMFORT SOME MIGHT FEEL, IN THE END, MANY PATIENTS ARE BETTER OFF WITHOUT OPIOIDS, EVEN IF IT MEANS MORE DISCOMFORT."[3]

—DR. JACQUELYN CORLEY, MD, DUKE UNIVERSITY PHYSICIAN

For several years, doctors and other medical professionals were caught in a difficult position. Many patients' bills are paid by the US government's Centers for Medicare & Medicaid Services (CMS). CMS aims to get its patients the best possible care. To assure this, patients are given surveys to rate the care they have received. Until 2017, the payments to hospitals were partially based on how well a patient's pain was managed. To score highly on the survey and keep the hospital financially stable, many doctors felt pressure to prescribe the highly effective opioids. Due to pressure and advocacy from physicians and medical organizations including the American Society of Anesthesiologists, pain management questions that rate the performance of hospitals still remain, but

PRESCRIPTION ABUSE

Emergency room physicians don't just treat opioid abusers—sometimes they become abusers themselves. Canadian physician Dr. Darryl Gebien became addicted to opioids in 2014 after abusing an old prescription of the opioid Percocet. This prescription was originally from a 2008 back injury. His life soon began to spiral out of control.

Gebien began to misuse his powers as a physician and wrote 445 false prescriptions. He used most of them for himself, but 35 were unaccounted for.[4] In January 2015, his actions were uncovered by investigators. He was sentenced to two years in prison but was released after just eight months. In 2018, Gebien was more than three years sober and used his story to raise awareness of the opioid crisis.

they are no longer directly tied to payments. CMS believes this will eliminate financial pressure physicians may feel to overprescribe pain medications.

Opioids are costly to patients, medical facilities, and society as a whole. The estimated cost of opioid use disorders and overdoses was $78 billion in 2013.[5] While that cost is extremely high, it is small compared with the overall economic effect of the opioid crisis. Societal and economic costs are also high because of crime associated with opioids.

THE LABOR FORCE

Research shows the opioid crisis costs the United States more than $500 billion per year. A research report from Princeton University demonstrates how opioids are contributing to a decline in the US labor force. The report estimated that from 1999 to 2015, 20 percent of the decline in the men's labor force was attributable to the opioid crisis.[6] During this time period, the number of men between the ages of 25 and 54 participating in the US labor force declined more than 3 percent.[7] Opioid prescriptions increased dramatically during that time frame. Researcher Alan B. Krueger discovered that between 1999 and 2015 there had also been a significant decrease in the labor force in other countries where increasing amounts of opioids were being prescribed.

Businesses are being hit hard by this labor shortage. CEO Michael Sherwin of Columbiana Boiler Company estimates his company loses $200,000 a year due to the lack of skilled workers. Qualified applicants have applied to his business, but nearly a quarter of them did not pass a drug test that includes screening for opioids.[8]

Unemployment can put strain on families.

A COPING MECHANISM

While opioid use is contributing to high unemployment, the reverse is also true. A 2017 study from the National Bureau of Economics examined this relationship. Findings showed that for every 1 percent increase in the unemployment rate, there was a 7 percent increase in opioid-related emergency room visits and a 3.6 percent increase in the opioid death rate.[9] Researchers believe this is linked to the increases in depression and other mental health problems that often occur during periods of economic decline.

Many opioid deaths are considered deaths of despair. Depression is often caused by a sudden change in economic conditions. As workers lose jobs, income, and sometimes their homes, depression and suicide rates go up. Many people have turned to opioids as a way to cope with their personal struggles or even end their lives.

If opioid addiction sets in, so can desperation. "You realize getting clean would be a lot of work," said Mady Ohlman, who struggled with opioid addiction. "And you realize dying would be a lot less painful. You also feel you'll

Law enforcement in rural areas is sometimes overwhelmed with fighting the opioid crisis.

be doing everyone else a favor if you die," she added.[10]

Ohlman was 22 when she attempted to commit suicide by opioid overdose. She had been addicted to opioids for three years. During that time, she stole from her mother and slept in her car. In 2018, Ohlman marked her fourth year of sobriety. She believed many other drug users have their will to live crushed by powerful addictions. This problem is reaching all corners of the United States.

TROUBLE IN RURAL AMERICA

There is a common misconception that drugs are most frequently abused by those living in the inner city. But poverty, lack of employment, and restricted access to social resources are compounding the drug abuse problem in rural areas. Rural communities are being hit hard by the opioid crisis. A 2017 survey indicated that 74 percent of farmers have been directly affected by the opioid crisis.[11] This is largely the result of a loss of capable workers. Local law enforcement agencies are also being strained by the demands opioids have caused. Rural New York Steuben County saw the number of opioid-related deaths triple in 2016. At this rate, rural law enforcement simply cannot keep up with the increasing problem.

Many rural communities are working within tight budgets and have difficulty attracting new businesses. If more local

TROUBLE IN NEW ORLEANS

"The opioid epidemic and the heroin trade it fuels has driven much of the violence we've seen in recent months," said New Orleans, Louisiana, police superintendent Michael Harrison.[12] In 2017, the city experienced an increase in gang violence. Law enforcement officials believe the violence is related to the opioid trade.

The source of the problems in New Orleans may not even be local. "I see the people who come in here to buy the [opioid] drugs," says New Orleans resident Lisa Fitzpatrick. "They drive cars that most people in my neighborhood can't afford. They're usually young, and seemingly well-off. They're not from my neighborhood. Some of them have out-of-state plates."[13] The city is being terrorized by violence caused in part by opioid seekers from other communities. While media coverage may focus on inner-city violence, the root cause may be coming from suburban or rural communities.

"YOU HAVE A SITUATION WHERE PEOPLE MIGHT BE PARTICULARLY VULNERABLE TO PERHAPS USING PRESCRIPTION OPIOIDS TO SELF-MEDICATE A LOT OF SYMPTOMS OF DISTRESS RELATED TO SOURCES OF CHRONIC STRESS."[14]

—DR. MAGDALENA CERDA, UNIVERSITY OF CALIFORNIA, DAVIS, EPIDEMIOLOGIST

resources are spent to combat the opioid crisis, it will become increasingly difficult for small towns to thrive. There is fear that the opioid crisis is bringing destruction to several rural communities. Small towns afflicted by the opioid crisis are entering a vicious cycle. As the local economy declines and criminal activity worsens, more people may try to leave the community or succumb to drug abuse. This creates even worse conditions that may lead to more illness, depression, and unemployment—all of which are potential reasons people decide to begin abusing opioids. If the cycle continues, the conditions will become more desperate.

Gangs have also become more prevalent in smaller communities. Some gangs move into these areas to push drugs, and others get their start in small towns as a way for members to escape poverty. Rural residents who deal with sickness, poverty, poor economic conditions, and depression may turn to these illegal organizations for a

In 2018, President Donald Trump gave a speech on how his administration would work to end the opioid crisis.

supply of drugs as a means of coping. Law enforcement officials believe this increase is happening because rural areas don't have the same resources to combat drug and gang activities that large cities do. This has been the case in rural Tennessee. There was a 14 percent increase in gang activity there between 2011 and 2016. Tennessee Bureau of Investigation director Mark Gwyn believes this spike is directly linked to the opioid crisis. He stated, "There's a big market in a lot of these small towns, too. There's a lot of people addicted."[15]

CHAPTER SIX

FINGER-POINTING

Emotions run high when a crisis causes so much harm, and the opioid epidemic is no exception. Individuals, families, and communities have been devastated by the harmful effects of opioids. As experts try to find solutions, they also work to discover the causes of the problems.

PHARMACY COMPANIES AND DISTRIBUTORS

Evidence suggests that large drug manufacturers and distributors played a significant role in the opioid crisis. Besides the fact that prescription opioids would not be widely available if these companies did not produce them, there have been examples of large pharmaceutical companies using deception to sell their products. Drug manufacturers that are under fire and

Doctors who overprescribe opioids share some of the blame for the opioid crisis.

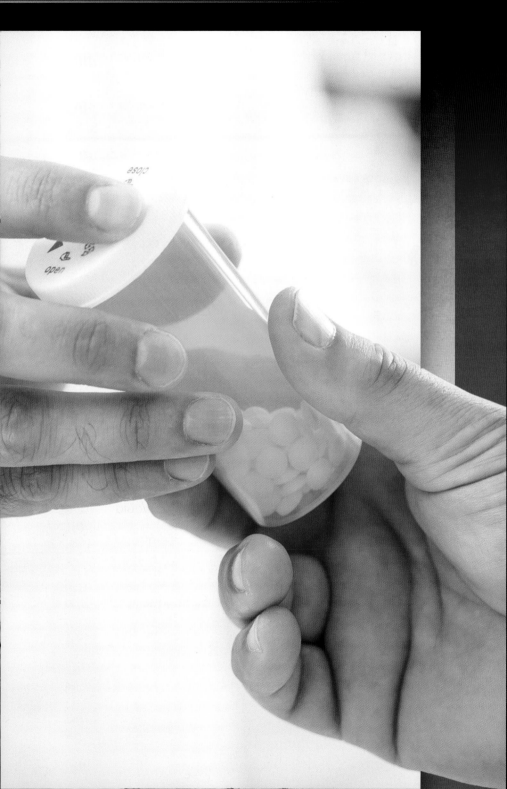

continue to face lawsuits include Purdue Pharma, Endo International, Teva Pharmaceutical Industries, Johnson & Johnson, and Allergan.

Purdue's problems have been well documented following its trial and fines in 2007. The company marketed OxyContin as having minimal addiction risk. This sales push suggested to doctors that opioids were not being prescribed enough. As a result, many physicians believed they were not treating their patients adequately. Opioids were viewed as a necessary tool for pain management. Despite contradictory medical evidence, Purdue publicly stood by claims that OxyContin provided 12 hours of pain relief. This led to higher sales because doctors believed that if relief didn't occur, the dose was too low. This push for higher opioid doses increased, despite a warning from the Centers for Disease Control and Prevention (CDC) that a higher dose leads to more potential for addiction and abuse.

Large distribution companies are facing pressure. These companies distribute opioids to hospitals and pharmacies nationwide. In a legal argument called the diversion theory, companies are legally supposed to stop distribution of controlled substances, such as opioids, if the company suspects misuse or illegal activity involving the drug. Some companies have chosen to ignore this problem despite clear evidence misuse is happening. Several of these companies either settled lawsuits in court or were forced to pay fines.

Large-scale production of prescription opioids likely couldn't occur without pharmaceutical companies. Without them, opioids would not be such powerful and widely distributed medications. However, unless they are stolen, these legal medications do not get to patients without a physician's prescription. Some argue doctors share the blame for the epidemic.

TOO MANY PILLS

Between 2006 and 2016, drug distributors sold more than 20 million opioid pills to pharmacies in the rural West Virginia community of Williamson. The town, located in Mingo County, had a population of 2,900 people. If handed out equally, that would have amounted to 7,172 pills for every resident.[1] Drug wholesale companies Miami-Luken and H. D. Smith are accused of needlessly flooding this community with opioid pills.

DOCTORS

Pain is a complex condition. The two main types of pain are acute and chronic. Acute pain typically arrives suddenly from a specific cause and usually doesn't last for more than six months. Surgery, broken bones, and burns are common sources of acute pain. Chronic pain lasts longer than six months. Pain can last far beyond the original injury, and sometimes it has no apparent cause. Common sources of chronic pain include arthritis and back pain. Doctors often see patients who have either chronic or acute pain.

The four vital signs doctors check when treating a patient are the patient's blood pressure, heart rate, respiratory rate, and temperature. In 1996, the American Pain Society declared pain to be the fifth vital sign. Any abnormal vital signs are required to be treated. Therefore, doctors believed it was necessary to aggressively treat pain.

Doctors who routinely overprescribe opioid medications are a common problem. Anesthesiologist Dr. Chad Brummett states, "There really aren't clear guidelines, especially for surgery and dentistry." He also says prescriptions for 45, 60, or 90 pills are common, even for minor surgeries.[2] In most cases, that amount is far too much for the patient.

Experts believe these large opioid prescriptions are dangerous. Unnecessarily large prescriptions leave extra pills available for abuse by anyone with access to them. In 2016, the CDC released guidelines to physicians stating opioid prescriptions for acute pain should not exceed seven days. However, applying the same standards for chronic pain could make access to prescribed medication more difficult for the patient.

ORGANIZATIONS AT FAULT

Some doctors believe an organization called the Joint Commission shares the blame for the opioid crisis. The Joint Commission is responsible for certifying tens of thousands of health organizations. Doctors and health-care administrators play by the commission's rules in order for their facilities to remain certified.

In 2001, the Joint Commission set new standards that require doctors to ask every hospital patient about his or her pain level. Much like the fifth vital sign movement, this led many doctors to believe they were not prescribing enough opioid pain medication. Since the new standards came out, the number of opioid prescriptions has skyrocketed.

Some doctors don't follow best practices or guidelines concerning opioids. There are examples of physicians looking to profit from the opioid crisis. These doctors run clinics nicknamed pill mills. Pill mills are notorious for overprescribing opioids. These doctors see an unusually high number of patients. Many of these patients don't medically need opioids. The more patients a doctor sees, the more money the doctor makes. From 1998 to 2018, 22 physicians either faced criminal charges or were convicted of inappropriately prescribing medicine.[3] Law enforcement agencies—including the FBI and DEA—locate and shut down pill mills.

DRUG CARTELS AND DEALERS

As the United States begins to crack down on the opioid crisis, it is becoming more difficult for people to obtain large amounts of prescription opioids. The most powerful opioid, fentanyl, is being created by Mexican drug cartels. These major criminal organizations have their own laboratories with specialized equipment. They are producing both fentanyl and heroin specifically for shipment to the United States.

Fentanyl isn't being sold to pharmacies or medical professionals. It's going straight into the hands of American gangs and drug dealers. Once gangs obtain fentanyl and heroin, the drugs are distributed across the United States. Illegal fentanyl has even reached as far as

Alaska. In 2017, 96 of the 128 overdose deaths in Alaska involved opioids. "It is a scary problem," says Alaska state trooper Captain Michael Duxbury. "Fentanyl is by far the biggest concern."[5]

Opioids and illegal drugs aren't just being sold on street corners. There is an illegal, online black market called the dark web. The dark web is only accessible by special software that is designed to make people untraceable online. A drug dealer in the United Kingdom was charged and sent to jail for eight years for using the dark web to sell and distribute fentanyl. Four people he was connected with died from opioid-related overdoses.

In 2016, New York authorities made a major drug bust. They showed news reporters the bags of heroin they seized.

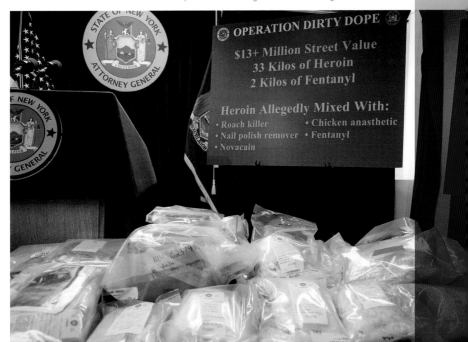

OPERATION DIRTY DOPE

$13+ Million Street Value
33 Kilos of Heroin
2 Kilos of Fentanyl

Heroin Allegedly Mixed With:
• Roach killer   • Chicken anasthetic
• Nail polish remover   • Fentanyl
• Novacain

This dealer illegally imported fentanyl from China and sent it to more than 100 people around the world.[6] The FBI is monitoring and busting similar transactions taking place in the United States. Dealers are getting more creative in drug sales, but they wouldn't be in business if they didn't have customers. Another source of fault for the crisis is the individual drug abuser.

PERSONAL RESPONSIBILITY

A research study was done in Australia to discover reasons why individuals chose to abuse opioids. One common motivator was to seek the pleasure caused by the drugs. Another reason was simply to relax after a stressful day. Instead of abusing illicit drugs, some people got similar effects by mixing prescribed painkillers with alcohol. In other cases, some people believed using opioids helped them better socialize with friends and family.

People also try to self-medicate by using opioids left over from old prescriptions. The pills are often obtained from someone else who had extra pills. Users feel relief from anxiety, depression, and physical pain after using these medications. A doctor's assessment is necessary to

Kids who find and use prescription drugs can develop addictions to opioids.

ensure a person is taking the correct dose for necessary medical reasons. It's never recommended that a person try to self-diagnose or treat these types of ailments by abusing drugs.

There is no one clear culprit for the opioid crisis. Rather than placing blame on a single cause, experts believe it's important that individuals, companies, and government agencies work together to develop effective and lasting solutions.

FROM THE
HEADLINES

FINDING FAKE PILL MILLS

Pill mills are clinics that notoriously overprescribe opioid medications. As bad as they are, fake pill mills are even more difficult to detect and shut down. These schemes occur when people illegally obtain prescription opioids with fake or otherwise invalid prescriptions. In 2018, a 46-year-old Philadelphia, Pennsylvania, man named David Francis Lawson was issued a series of felony charges. His charges included acquiring controlled substances by fraud, forgery, deception, misrepresentation, and other methods.

He is accused of running a ring of illegal drug sales that included ten other people. Investigators believe this pill mill organization used home computers, prescription paper, and information stolen from doctors to make hundreds of fake prescriptions. The result of this activity led to Lawson and his team obtaining more than 12,600 pills of oxycodone, with the intent to resell in southeastern Pennsylvania.[7]

Lawson's scheme involved selling the counterfeit prescriptions to other members of his group in exchange for $250 and a portion of the obtained opioid pills. He then sold these leftover

Law enforcement officials in Miami, Florida, are cracking down on fake pill mills.

pills on the street to unknown people. This allowed him to make even more money. A pharmacist in Philadelphia noticed an unusually large increase in opioid prescriptions from a certain doctor. This led the pharmacist to contact the authorities in 2016. The DEA soon became involved. "Thanks to strong law enforcement collaboration, this fraudulent prescription drug mill was shut down," proclaimed Pennsylvania attorney general Josh Shapiro.[8]

CHAPTER SEVEN

MEDICAL AND
THERAPEUTIC
TREATMENTS

There is still a lot of work to be done to solve the opioid crisis. However, there are promising medical and therapeutic techniques that bring people back from overdoses, opioid abuse, and opioid addiction.

Naloxone is one drug that can save people experiencing opioid overdoses. If administered quickly enough, naloxone blocks and reverses the impact of opioids. Many first responders and medical professionals are trained to use naloxone. "With this reversal agent, we're saving the vast majority of

As the opioid crisis continues, more first responders are carrying naloxone in case they need to treat opioid overdoses.

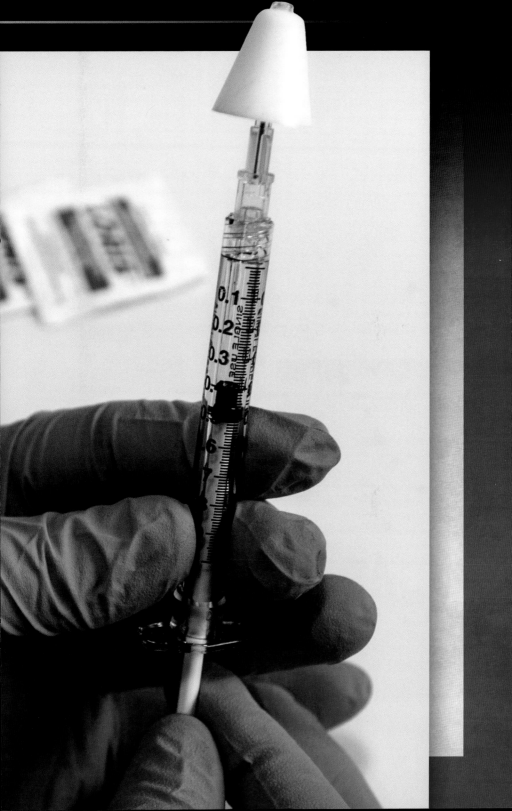

people," said emergency room physician Scott Weiner. A study from 2013 to 2015 showed naloxone to be 93.5 percent effective for reversing opioid overdoses.[1] Current laws allow anyone with proper training to administer the drug—including family members of people struggling with opioid addictions.

Between 1996 and 2014, people who were not medical professionals reversed more than 26,500 overdoses using naloxone.[2] Naloxone has rescued many lives and promises to save countless more. Unfortunately, overdoses are only one part of the problem. The ideal situation is to prevent overdoses before they happen. Treatment for addiction and abuse is one way to prevent overdoses.

CONTROVERSIAL TREATMENT

Advocates for an herb called kratom claim this plant helps combat opioid addiction. Chemicals within the plant relieve pain and serve as an alternative to opioids. However, kratom's effect on the brain has the DEA concerned. In 2018, the DEA considered a federal ban on kratom as it has contributed to substance abuse and deaths. But kratom advocate Susan Ash argues, "They [the US government] need to recognize the millions of us who are using this responsibly and getting off opiates."[3]

MEDICAL TREATMENTS

NIDA believes medical treatment for opioid addiction and abuse is highly effective but underutilized. Medications that have been proven to treat opioid use disorder include methadone, buprenorphine, and naltrexone.

Methadone works by preventing withdrawal and blocking the effects of opioids if they are used. It is dispensed daily to the patient by an approved clinic. The drug acts like other opioids, but it reaches the brain more slowly than other similar drugs. This effect makes the high a patient feels from abused opioids seem lower. It has been around since the 1960s and still remains an effective addiction solution.

Buprenorphine is a medication that prevents the craving for opioids. The medication is typically taken orally and does not require daily dispensing from a medical professional. This factor makes buprenorphine more widely available for people who need it. In 2016, the Food and Drug Administration (FDA) approved a small implantable version of buprenorphine that can be placed under the skin. This implant provides six months of slow-releasing medication. In 2017, the FDA approved a once-monthly injectable version of buprenorphine as well. Longer-lasting medications have allowed more patients to stick with opioid treatment programs.

DECIDING TO HEAL

Actor Robert Downey Jr.'s struggle with addiction is perhaps one of the greatest recovery success stories in Hollywood. Downey is known for playing Iron Man in the Marvel movie blockbusters. From an early age, he was given alcohol and other drugs by his father, which contributed to a long period of abuse.

Downey was arrested many times for possession of heroin, cocaine, and marijuana. In the early 2000s, he found himself in and out of rehab. In 2003, his then fiancée Susan Levin warned that she would leave him unless he fully committed to changing his ways. He committed to becoming sober and married Levin in 2005.

During a 2004 interview on *The Oprah Winfrey Show*, the actor said, "It's really not that difficult to overcome these seemingly ghastly problems. . . . What's hard is to decide."[4] Since sticking to his recovery, Downey has gone on to become one of the highest paid and most recognizable actors in the world.

BEHAVIORAL THERAPY

Another method of treatment is often used with or without medication. It focuses on changing the behaviors of people with opioid addictions. Reinforcing people's good behavior helps their minds create healthy habits. Offering an incentive for quitting opioids has been shown to have a positive influence. An incentive helps keep patients in treatment and promotes healthy lifestyles.

One incentive-based method is called voucher-based reinforcement (VBR). The practice of VBR includes rewarding individuals who stay drug free. For every drug-free urine sample provided, the person receives a voucher that is exchanged for movie

Ashley Gardner travels two hours from her home to get methadone at a clinic in Georgia.

passes, food, and other healthful goods or services. The value of the vouchers, which is at first low, progressively increases, giving patients a positive reason to continue the treatment program. If a sample comes back testing positive for drugs, the value of the voucher resets to the original low amount. The voucher program has been shown to be an effective technique for helping people overcome opioid addiction.

Cognitive behavioral therapy (CBT) is also a helpful treatment technique. In CBT, therapists work with patients to identify and address negative thought patterns. This therapy helps patients respond to difficult situations, such as drug triggers, in healthy ways.

Both medical and behavioral therapies have shown effectiveness against opioid addiction. These treatments have a place in society for the foreseeable future. Helping patients overcome substance abuse reduces the number of people with addictions. Individuals are at the heart of the opioid crisis, and getting them the help they need is an important step in battling the opioid epidemic. Many believe this is part of the compassionate method for handling people battling substance abuse. Advocates of this approach argue that much of the crisis can be solved through kindness, understanding, and proper therapeutic techniques. The United States has traditionally punished drug abusers, as addiction was often considered a moral failing rather than a chronic disease.

With both medical and behavioral treatment, patients often have a choice between outpatient and inpatient treatment. Outpatient treatment allows a person to

INEFFECTIVE
TREATMENT CENTERS

Millions of dollars are spent every year on opioid addiction treatment. The dollar amount has increased nearly 1,000 percent from 2010 to 2015. In 2018, there were more than 14,000 addiction treatment programs in the United States.[6] Not all of these facilities are equally effective. There is possible widespread financial abuse in the addiction treatment industry. Many treatment centers operate more like five-star luxury resorts than medical facilities.

"Often times, poor rehab programs offer nice amenities in a scenic location, but lack the appropriate clinical care," says Spectrum Health System vice president of clinical services Lisa Blanchard. She adds, "They have great mattresses, HD TVs, and horseback riding, but these programs usually suffer from inadequate staffing combined with a lack of clear recovery programming."[7] There are many treatment centers taking insurance money and not giving patients the help they need.

freely live at home and travel to and from a treatment facility for care. Inpatient treatment requires patients to live in a treatment facility, sometimes for days or weeks at a time. Inpatient care may be preferred by someone who is at high risk of re-abusing opioids at home or in the community.

WHY IS TREATMENT NOT ALWAYS ENOUGH?

A patient must want to receive treatment for it to be most effective. A survey from the Substance Abuse and Mental Health Services Administration found approximately 90 percent of people who need drug rehab do not receive it.[8] New people become addicted every day, and treatments are not always effective. Highly effective treatments slow the crisis, but they do not necessarily stop it.

The Betty Ford Center is one well-known treatment facility in California.

Cartels, drug dealers, and pill mills still push for profit, as their actions show more care for making money than the health of society. Increased success in treatments that help some users recover potentially causes these groups to push harder for new users and become more violent in the process. Drug manufacturers and distributors need to be responsible for inappropriate or illegal actions too. Individual treatments do not necessarily solve these other problems. This is where government and law enforcement agencies step in.

CHAPTER EIGHT

CRIME, RACE, AND PUNISHMENT

The explosion of opioid use, abuse, and addiction has led to significant increases in criminal activity. Many users turn to illegal sources of opioids to fight off or prevent withdrawal. This has led to a surge of heroin use in the United States. The criminal black-market economy for heroin and other opioid drugs is booming. Drug dealers are enriching themselves off of people who have become addicted to opioids and those who want to experiment with or abuse opioids.

Black men typically get longer jail sentences than white men for the same crime.

Meanwhile, thousands of drug dealers' customers die as a result of opioid overdoses. Many dealers are charged with crimes. In criminal cases involving known deaths, dealers are often charged with manslaughter, which is the unintentional killing of another human. In 2018, a prison sentence was handed down to a drug dealer in New York. His heroin and fentanyl combination was proven to have killed at least one person. He was sentenced to more than ten years in prison.

In some cases, even possessing illegal drugs leads to significant punishment. Between 1993 and 2011, there were millions of arrests in the United States for drug possession. Many were related to heroin and other opioids. While possession likely won't lead to significant prison time, repeat offenders and distributors sometimes face life

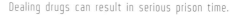

Dealing drugs can result in serious prison time.

in prison. Experts believe this has led to a high financial burden for taxpayers and fewer opportunities in life for the people who are prosecuted.

Heroin use does not necessarily create violent behavior, but the opioid crisis has certainly contributed to violent acts. When going through withdrawal, a person with an addiction will sometimes resort to violence to obtain money, goods, or the drugs themselves. Gangs and drug dealers use violence and murder to gain advantages over rivals. Criminal drug organizations, called cartels, are responsible for illegally exporting heroin into the United States from Mexico. Cartels are notorious for committing extreme acts of violence to remain in power. These cartels have a significant presence in the United States, including operations with gangs. The gang most commonly associated with cartels is called MS-13. US attorney general Jeff Sessions has considered the possibility of designating the violent MS-13 gang a terrorist organization.

CARTEL CRACKDOWN

Mexican cartels are doing everything possible to increase the flow of heroin and other drugs into the United States.

MORE TO THE
STORY

WHAT IS MS-13?

A violent gang in the United States named Mara Salvatrucha, also known as MS-13, started in the early 1980s in Los Angeles, California. Its members were immigrants from Mexico, as well as El Salvador, Honduras, Guatemala, and other Central and South American countries. The group has since spread across the United States. It heavily recruits middle school and high school students from immigrant communities. Members are threatened with violence if they choose to leave the gang.

Between 2016 and 2018, MS-13 was believed to be responsible for 25 killings on Long Island in New York.[1] The group is also working with Mexican cartels to funnel illegal opioids into the black market. In his 2018 State of the Union address, President Donald Trump personally addressed family members of those affected by MS-13 violence. He stated, "We cannot imagine the depth of your sorrow, but we can make sure that other families never have to endure this pain."[2] As of 2018, new legislation was being developed to provide resources to combat and crack down on this violent gang.

The majority of all heroin comes to the United States from Mexico. As several US states legalized marijuana, cartels saw a decrease in marijuana profits. US Customs and Border Protection reports show that since 2012, marijuana seizures, or confiscation by authorities, have been cut in half, likely due to fewer illegal imports. During the same time, heroin and methamphetamine seizures have dramatically increased.

The fight against drugs being smuggled into the United States involves several tactics. The first method is cooperation with foreign governments. The US and Mexican governments are working together on a project called the Merida Initiative. Beginning in 2008, through the Merida Initiative, the United States provided resources to help reform Mexico's police force, military, and court systems. Through training, equipment, and updated facilities, the United States hopes the Mexican government is now better equipped to take on cartels and drug runners.

Another idea to stop drugs from entering the United States has experts, politicians, and the country divided. President Donald Trump and his supporters believe a solution to stopping the influx of illegal immigration and drug trafficking is a physical barrier: a wall along the US-Mexico border. Others believe building a wall won't have any effect. Some experts see it as part of a comprehensive plan to manage the influx of smuggled goods but not the entire solution.

DEALING WITH THE DEALERS

According to the FBI, there are more than 33,000 gangs in the United States. These organizations are made up of nearly 1.4 million members.[3] Violence is a gang's go-to method for making illegal activities easier. The FBI has

Joaquin "El Chapo" Guzman, a Mexican drug lord, was arrested in 2014 by Mexican authorities. His US trial was scheduled for late 2018. He was charged in part for importing heroin and other drugs into the country.

dedicated significant resources to cracking down on violent gangs and drug dealers.

In 2005, the FBI was directed by Congress to create the National Gang Intelligence Center (NGIC). The NGIC brings together information from federal, state, and local law enforcement agencies. This information allows the NGIC and other authorities to identify and target the most dangerous gangs in the country.

Combining federal and local agencies has been a successful technique for cracking down on opioid traffickers. The Tampa Police Department in Tampa, Florida, began a partnership with the FBI to take on heroin-related gang violence in 2015. One gang they targeted was led by Felix Mejia Lagunas. To follow the activity of Lagunas's gang, the agencies used techniques such as recording undercover drug purchases, using physical and electronic surveillance, reviewing financial records, and intercepting mail that contained drugs or cash.

The collected evidence led to a major bust. In 2017,

"WE HAVE ALREADY INFILTRATED THEIR [CRIMINALS'] NETWORKS, AND WE ARE DETERMINED TO BRING THEM TO JUSTICE."[4]

—JEFF SESSIONS, US ATTORNEY GENERAL, SPEAKING ON DISRUPTING THE OPIOID CRISIS

investigators raided homes, storage units, and other locations associated with Lagunas's gang. Investigators recovered bags of heroin, nine firearms, and $600,000 in cash. That dollar amount was believed to be the average daily profit from the gang's drug sales. All 16 gang members pleaded guilty, including Lagunas, who oversaw the gang's activities from his home in California. In 2017, Lagunas was sentenced to 27 years in federal prison.[5]

RACE AND DRUGS

There is significant evidence demonstrating that African Americans and whites don't receive similar treatment when it comes to medicine, media coverage, and law enforcement in response to the opioid crisis and overall war on drugs.

In Illinois, African Americans accounted for 15 percent of the state's population but were victims of nearly a quarter of all opioid deaths in 2016.[6] Making the situation worse, some Illinois clinics that predominantly served African Americans lacked buprenorphine—a critical addiction-treatment medication. Absence of effective treatment may have been a factor in the 2016 doubling of the overdose death rate in Illinois's African American population.

During the 1980s and 1990s, the United States aggressively pursued a war on drugs. Hundreds of thousands of people ended up in prison for drug-related crimes. The country spent a significant amount of money on the campaign, which did almost nothing to reduce addiction rates. African Americans were disproportionately placed in prison and received harsher sentences than whites for the same crimes. From 1980 to 1997, the number of nonviolent drug offenders in prison rose from 50,000 to more than 400,000.[7] A 2015 report by the US Department of Justice showed that the majority of people in federal prison for drug offenses are Latino or African American.

CHAPTER NINE

WHAT'S NEXT?

T he opioid crisis is gaining attention nationwide. The possible causes of this crisis are being put under a microscope by the government and media. The medical community is reevaluating how opioids are dispensed, and new research is finding effective treatment solutions. Society is beginning to realize the depth and darkness of the opioid epidemic.

FEDERAL HELP

In 2017, President Trump declared the opioid crisis a "public health emergency."[1] The US Department of Health and Human Services outlined a five-point strategy to combat the opioid crisis. The strategy

Police have K-9 units that help sniff out drugs in vehicles.

outlined ways the federal government would use resources to provide evidence-based solutions.

The first strategy is to improve access to prevention, treatment, and recovery services. The second point is to increase the availability of overdose-reversal medications, such as naloxone, especially in high-risk areas. The next goal is to improve public health data collection and reporting. These help track the epidemic as it evolves. The fourth point is to support research that develops alternatives to opioid pain medication and ways to reduce opioid-related health damages. The fifth goal is to advance pain management practices by finding ways to simultaneously relieve pain and reduce inappropriate use of opioids.

In the 2018 government budget, Congress received billions of dollars to directly address the opioid crisis. In February 2018, a group of US senators from both major parties released a bill that

ADDED SECURITY

On January 10, 2018, President Trump signed a bill into law that provided millions of dollars for specialized equipment that detects fentanyl and other opioids crossing US borders. Chemical screening devices will be implemented at checkpoints and stations where foreign mail is screened. Fentanyl is often sent to Mexico and Canada from China, then sent to the United States through the postal service.

addressed the opioid problem. As of June 2018, the bill had not yet passed. The bill is one of the most significant pieces of legislation addressing the opioid epidemic. The bill includes six major changes.

The first measure is to limit initial opioid prescriptions to three days, with the exception of cancer treatment and end-of-life care. The second goal is to allow nurse practitioners and physician assistants to prescribe the treatment medication buprenorphine. A third measure is to require physicians to use drug monitoring programs that allow doctors to see whether patients are already receiving opioids from other facilities.

The proposed bill also requires the federal government to develop national standards for recovery housing. Standards help ensure patients will receive appropriate and safe care. The fifth major measure is to increase penalties for manufacturers that don't report suspicious orders of opioids. The last goal is to provide significant

MONITORING PATIENTS

Researchers are developing opioid medications with radio transmitters built inside. When a patient takes a pill, a sensor is triggered by stomach acid and sends a message to the doctor. This tells the doctor that an opioid pill has been taken. The information is being used to track how many pills are being taken and how often. This data collection has the potential to help set guidelines for more appropriate and effective prescriptions.

financial resources for treatment. It authorizes $1 billion to expand access to medical treatment and equip more first responders with naloxone.[2] This $1 billion also provides recovery services for veterans, pregnant and postpartum women, and other vulnerable people.

MEDICAL ASSESSMENT

Information from a 2018 study from the *Journal of the American Medical Association* has the potential to revolutionize the way chronic pain is managed. Chronic pain is one of the most common reasons opioids are prescribed. Some of these patients end up abusing or becoming addicted to the opioid medications. The assumption made by many physicians is that opioids are a more effective treatment solution than non-opioid drugs.

Back pain is one type of chronic pain.

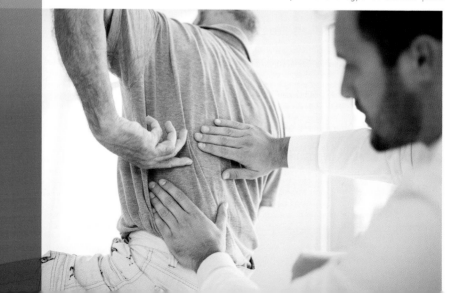

In this research study, patients with chronic pain were randomly assigned a variety of pain medications. Some received the opioid drugs Vicodin, oxycodone, and fentanyl. Others received a variety of non-opioids, which included Tylenol, ibuprofen, and other types of prescription nerve and muscle pain medications.

The research group was made up of hundreds of patients from Minneapolis, Minnesota, Veterans Affairs clinics. The patients' habits and medical records were tracked for one year. The results came as a surprise to doctors, patients, and others following the opioid crisis. Non-opioid

"I THINK PEOPLE NEED TO BE AWARE THAT IF THEY'RE GIVEN AN OPTION FOR OPIOIDS, THEY SHOULD ASK TO TRY NON-OPIOID OPTIONS."[4]

—DR. TARA NARULA

medications proved slightly more effective than opioids for managing chronic pain. "This is a very important study," said Dr. David Reuben of the University of California, Los Angeles. "It will likely change the approach to managing long-term back, hip and knee pain."[3]

Non-opioid medications do come with their own problems. The active drug in Tylenol is called acetaminophen. Acetaminophen can cause liver damage with an overdose or with regular use—especially if paired with alcohol. Significant overuse of another common pain reliever, ibuprofen, and other pain medications causes an inflammation of the stomach called gastritis. This condition needs close monitoring. Gastritis has the potential to cause bleeding in the stomach and create ulcers.

This study could change the standards and direction doctors take for treating both chronic and acute pain.

DRUG TRANSITION

Researchers are exploring ways to get patients off of opioid medications. One possible solution is another controversial drug: medical marijuana. The Minnesota Department of Health studied opioid-prescribed patients who began using marijuana for chronic pain. The majority of the studied patients using medical marijuana were able to reduce or eliminate opioid use after six months. A 2016 study from Michigan produced similar results. The study reported that having access to marijuana treatment "was associated with a 64 percent decrease in opioid use, decreased number and side effects of medications, and an improved quality of life."[5]

There is a wide variety of non-opioid medications. If one doesn't work, a doctor may prescribe another before making the leap to opioids. Other studies show physical therapy and exercise to be the most effective treatment for chronic pain. Someday, opioids could become an afterthought for medical treatment. That has the potential to turn the tide against the epidemic.

COMMUNITY HELP

Numerous nonprofit organizations are trying to be agents of change in the fight against opioid abuse and addiction. An organization called RIZE Massachusetts is bringing together many large private companies. It aims to establish a fund that will be used to create opioid-related programs from prevention to recovery.

In 2016, the organization Advocates for Opioid Recovery was created by civil rights activist Van Jones and former politicians. This group's mission is to educate influential leaders on the effectiveness of medication-based treatment. It aims to help create sustainable and effective solutions through new laws.

There is promising progress being made toward overcoming the opioid crisis. Innovative problem-solving and collaboration is pointing lawmakers, medical professionals, and law enforcement toward meaningful solutions. Since there is no single fix to such a complex situation, much work is still needed.

ESSENTIAL
FACTS

MAJOR EVENTS

- Opioid-like drugs have been around for centuries and were used around the world before causing a crisis in the United States.

- Opioids have a dramatic effect on the brain, which makes them highly desirable and hard to quit. Opioids can also cause significant damage to the rest of the body. Hundreds of thousands of people have fallen victim to opioid overdoses.

- A medication called naloxone has saved thousands of lives. Other medications can be used to treat people trying to recover from opioid addiction. Behavioral therapy is also commonly used for addiction recovery and other issues that may lead to drug use.

- Large drug busts have occurred from coast to coast, including one that seized enough fentanyl to kill 18 million people. Local law enforcement agencies are teaming up with federal authorities to crack down on criminal gangs and stop the flood of deadly drugs from foreign cartels.

KEY PLAYERS

- Gangs and cartels bring opioids into the United States and distribute them throughout the nation.

- Researchers are releasing studies that may forever change the way doctors prescribe painkillers.

- In 2017, the US Department of Health and Human Services outlined ways the federal government can combat the opioid crisis.

- Advocates for Opioid Recovery was founded in 2016 to help educate US leaders on medication-based treatment for people with addictions.

IMPACT ON SOCIETY

Approximately one person dies from an opioid overdose every eight minutes. This epidemic is destroying lives, tearing families apart, and placing a large strain on medical resources, the criminal justice system, and the national economy.

QUOTE

"The big moneymaker right now, given the opioid epidemic, is heroin, and the reason that it's heroin is that people who have become addicted to prescription opioids find it a lot cheaper to purchase heroin."

—Mike Vigil, *former chief of internal operations at the DEA*

GLOSSARY

COGNITIVE
Related to the act or process of thinking, reasoning, remembering, imagining, or learning.

DERIVATIVE
Something that is based on another source.

EPIDEMIC
The widespread occurrence of something negative.

FELONY
A crime more serious than a misdemeanor, usually punishable by imprisonment.

INFLUX

The arrival or entry of a large number of people or things.

MONOPOLIZE

To create exclusive control over a commodity or service.

NEUROTRANSMITTER

A brain chemical that helps brain cells communicate with other brain cells.

POSTPARTUM

Occurring or being in the time following childbirth.

SYNTHETIC

Something made by combining chemicals, typically to imitate a natural product.

VOUCHER

A piece of paper or receipt that can be exchanged for goods or services.

ADDITIONAL
RESOURCES

SELECTED BIBLIOGRAPHY

"Opioid Overdose Crisis." *National Institute on Drug Abuse*, Mar. 2018, drugabuse.gov. Accessed 18 June 2018.

"Opium throughout History." *PBS*, n.d., pbs.org. Accessed 18 June 2018.

"What Are the Treatments for Heroin Addiction?" *National Institute on Drug Abuse*, n.d., drugabuse.gov. Accessed 18 June 2018.

FURTHER READINGS

Abramovitz, Melissa. *Brain Science*. Abdo, 2016.

Abramovitz, Melissa. *Heroin and Prescription Opioids*. Abdo, 2019.

Newton, David E. *Prescription Drug Abuse*. ABC-CLIO, 2015.

ONLINE RESOURCES

Booklinks
NONFICTION NETWORK
FREE! ONLINE NONFICTION RESOURCES

To learn more about the opioid crisis, visit **abdobooklinks.com**.
These links are routinely monitored and updated to provide
the most current information available.

MORE INFORMATION

For more information on this subject, contact or visit the
following organizations:

Drug Enforcement Administration Museum and Visitors Center
700 Army Navy Drive
Arlington, VA 22202
202-307-3463
deamuseum.org
The DEA Museum offers education on the history of the DEA and the
impact of past, present, and future drug addiction.

National Institute on Drug Abuse
6001 Executive Boulevard
Room 5213, MSC 9561
Bethesda, MD 20892
301-443-1124
drugabuse.gov
The National Institute on Drug Abuse offers a wealth of information on
the opioid crisis and many other drugs that are abused.

SOURCE
NOTES

CHAPTER 1. TRAGEDY STRIKES

1. Lynda Kinkade. "Opioid Crisis: Childhood Friends Die on Same Day, Half a Mile Apart." *CNN*, 1 Dec. 2017, cnn.com. Accessed 22 June 2018.

2. "Governor Ducey Declares Statewide Health Emergency in Opioid Epidemic." *Center for Rural Health*, n.d., crh.arizona.edu. Accessed 22 June 2018.

3. Ronald H Spector. "Vietnam War." *Encyclopædia Britannica*, n.d., britannica.com. Accessed 22 June 2018.

4. "Overdose Death Rates." *National Institute on Drug Abuse*, Sept. 2017, drugabuse.gov. Accessed 22 June 2018.

5. Kinkade, "Opioid Crisis."

6. "What Is Fentanyl?" *National Institute on Drug Abuse*, June 2016, drugabuse.gov. Accessed 22 June 2018.

7. "Opioid Overdose Crisis." *National Institute on Drug Abuse*, Mar. 2018, drugabuse.gov. Accessed 22 June 2018.

8. Christopher Woody. "Mexican Heroin Is Flooding the US, and the Sinaloa Cartel Is Steering the Flow." *Business Insider*, 18 Nov. 2017, businessinsider.com. Accessed 22 June 2018.

9. "Overdose Death Rates."

10. OMI. "Big Data Reveals 1 Out of 6 ER Visits In Q2 2017 Opioid Related." *PR Newswire*, 27 Nov. 2017, prnewswire.com. Accessed 22 June 2018.

11. "Overdose Death Rates."

12. Drake Baer. "The American Opioid Epidemic Is a Crisis of Meaning." *Medium*, 1 June 2017, medium.com. Accessed 22 June 2018.

13. Dan Diamond. "First There Was Prince. Now Tom Petty. When Will America Finally Wake Up to the Opioid Crisis?" *Politico Magazine*, 20 Jan. 2018, politico.com. Accessed 22 June 2018.

14. Macklemore. "Macklemore: Compassion Can Help Country Fight Opioid Crisis." *Time*, 22 Feb. 2018, time.com. Accessed 22 June 2018.

15. Sarah Jorgensen. "Fentanyl Seizure Had Enough Doses to Poison all of NYC and New Jersey." *CNN*, 29 Jan. 2018, cnn.com. Accessed 22 June 2018.

CHAPTER 2. THE HISTORY OF OPIOIDS

1. Nick Miroff. "From Teddy Roosevelt to Trump: How Drug Companies Triggered an Opioid Crisis a Century Ago." *Washington Post*, 17 Oct. 2017, washingtonpost.com. Accessed 22 June 2018.

2. "Heroin by Area of Origin." *Heroin.net*, n.d., heroin.net. Accessed 22 June 2018.

3. "Heroin by Area of Origin."

4. Art Van Zee. "The Promotion and Marketing of OxyContin: Commercial Triumph, Public Health Tragedy." *American Journal of Public Health*, vol. 99, no. 1, 2009, pp. 221–227.

CHAPTER 3. THE SCIENCE OF THE CRISIS

1. "Opioids." *National Institute on Drug Abuse*, n.d., drugabuse.gov. Accessed 22 June 2018.

2. Stephanie Pappas. "Massive Poppy Bust: Why Home-Grown Opium Is Rare." *LiveScience*, 12 June 2017. livescience.com. Accessed 22 June 2018.

CHAPTER 4. THE EFFECTS ON INDIVIDUALS

1. Jen Christensen. "How Heroin Kills You." *CNN*, 19 Aug. 2015, cnn.com. Accessed 22 June 2018.

2. "The Science of Addiction: Breaking the Stigma." *AddictionCenter*, 17 July 2015, addictioncenter.com. Accessed 22 June 2018.

3. Cole Waterman. "'I've Literally Ruined My Life:' Bay City Heroin Addict Shares His Story Amid Overdose Epidemic." *MLive*, 11 July 2018, mlive.com. Accessed 22 June 2018.

4. "Drug Use and Viral Infections (HIV, Hepatitis)." *National Institute on Drug Abuse*, Apr. 2018, drugabuse.gov. Accessed 22 June 2018.

5. Kathleen Smith. "Depression and Opioid Abuse: How Painkillers Affect Your Mental Health." *Psycom*, 13 Feb. 2018, psycom.net. Accessed 22 June 2018.

6. Sandra Gurvis. "Health: A Mother's Story about the Opioid Crisis." *Columbus Monthly*, 27 Feb. 2018, columbusmonthly.com. Accessed 22 June 2018.

7. Gurvis, "Health: A Mother's Story."

8. "Homelessness and Housing." *SAMHSA*, 15 Sept. 2017, samhsa.gov. Accessed 22 June 2018.

9. "Overdose Deaths among Homeless Persons." *National Institute on Drug Abuse*, Jan. 2013, drugabuse.gov. Accessed 22 June 2018.

10. Ellis, Ralph. "Tom Petty Died of Accidental Drug Overdose, Medical Examiner Says." *CNN*, 21 Jan. 2018, cnn.com. Accessed 22 June 2018.

CHAPTER 5. SOCIAL COSTS

1. Audrey Weiss, et al. "Opioid-Related Inpatient Stays and Emergency Department Visits by State, 2009–2014." *Healthcare Cost and Utilization Project*, Jan. 2017, hcup-us.ahrq.gov. Accessed 22 June 2018.

2. Alice Yin. "Health Care Professionals Share Their Stories about Opioid-Addicted Patients." *New York Times*, 13 Feb. 2018, nytimes.com. Accessed 22 June 2018.

3. Dr. Jacquelyn Corley. "To Fix the Opioid Crisis, Doctors Like Me May Have to Let Patients Be in Pain." *NBC News*, 9 Jan. 2018, nbcnews.com. Accessed 22 June 2018.

4. "Former ER Doctor Who Wrote Fake Fentanyl Prescriptions Sentenced to 2 Years in Prison." *CTV News*, 19 Apr. 2017, ctvnews.ca. Accessed 22 June 2018.

5. "How Much Does Opioid Treatment Cost?" *National Institute on Drug Abuse*, Jan. 2018, drugabuse.gov. Accessed 22 June 2018.

6. Alan B. Krueger. "Where Have All the Workers Gone? An Inquiry into the Decline of the U.S. Labor Force Participation Rate." *Brookings*, 7 Sept. 2017, brookings.edu. Accessed 22 June 2018.

SOURCE NOTES
CONTINUED

7. "Labor Force Participation: What Has Happened Since the Peak?" *Bureau of Labor Statistics*, Sept. 2016, bls.gov. Accessed 22 June 2018.

8. Nicholas Wyman. "America's Workforce Is Paying a Huge Price for the Opioid Epidemic." *Forbes*, 12 Dec. 2017, forbes.com. Accessed 22 June 2018.

9. Olga Khazan. "The Link between Opioids and Unemployment." *Atlantic*, 18 Apr. 2017, theatlantic.com. Accessed 22 June 2018.

10. Martha Bebinger. "How Many Opioid Overdoses Are Suicides?" *KHN*, 28 Mar. 2018, khn.org. Accessed 22 June 2018.

11. "Opioid Misuse in Rural America." *USDA*, n.d., usda.gov. Accessed 22 June 2018.

12. Nick Valencia. "Gangs, Opioids Fueling Spate of Violence in New Orleans, Police Say." *CNN*, 20 June 2017, cnn.com. Accessed 22 June 2018.

13. Valencia, "Gangs, Opioids Fueling Spate of Violence."

14. Luke Runyon. "Why Is the Opioid Epidemic Hitting Rural American Especially Hard?" *NPR Illinois*, 4 Jan. 2017, nprillinois.org. Accessed 22 June 2018.

15. Adam Tamburin. "Gangs and Cartels Are Teaming Up to Bring Drugs into Rural Tennessee, TBI Director Says." *Tennessean*, 22 Nov. 2017, tennessean.com. Accessed 22 June 2018.

CHAPTER 6. FINGER-POINTING

1. Emma Roller. "Big Pharma Peddled 780 Million Opioids to West Virginia over the Past Six Years." *Splinter*, 30 Jan. 2018, splinternews.com. Accessed 22 June 2018.

2. Michelle Andrews. "Questioning a Doctor's Prescription for a Sore Knee: 90 Percocets." *NPR*, 22 Nov. 2017, npr.org. Accessed 22 June 2018.

3. Megan Luther. "Doctors across the U.S. are Over Prescribing Opioids, Running Pill Mills." *Independent Online*, 27 Feb. 2018, dailyindependent.com. Accessed 22 June 2018.

4. "Drug Dealer Jailed for Using the Dark Web to Supply Powerful Opioid Fentanyl." *ITV*, 5 Feb. 2018, itv.com. Accessed 22 June 2018.

5. Rachel D'Oro. "Alaska Troopers: Fentanyl Overdoses Are a Growing Concern." *PoliceOne*, 14 Feb. 2018, policeone.com. Accessed 22 June 2018.

6. "Drug Dealer Jailed for Using the Dark Web to Supply Powerful Opioid Fentanyl."

7. "10 People Charged for Re-Selling Opioids Obtained from Fake Prescriptions." *Fox43*, 28 Feb. 2018, fox43.com. Accessed 22 June 2018.

8. "10 People Charged for Re-Selling Opioids."

CHAPTER 7. MEDICAL AND THERAPEUTIC TREATMENTS

1. Nadia Kounang. "Naloxone Reverses 93% of Overdoses." *CNN*, 30 Oct. 2017, cnn.com. Accessed 22 June 2018.

2. "Naloxone for Opioid Overdose: Life-Saving Science." *National Institute on Drug Abuse*, Mar. 2017, drugabuse.gov. Accessed 22 June 2018.

3. Frank Main. "Kratom, Health Supplement Targeted by FDA, Linked to 9 Deaths in Cook County." *Chicago Sun Times*, 5 Mar. 2018, chicago.suntimes.com. Accessed 22 June 2018.

4. "The Comeback Kid." *Oprah*, 23 Nov. 2004, oprah.com. Accessed 22 June 2018.

5. Sheila Kaplan. "F.D.A. to Expand Medication-Assisted Therapy for Opioid Addicts." *New York Times*, 25 Feb. 2018, nytimes.com. Accessed 22 June 2018.

6. Mari Edlin. "Scammers, Fraudsters Capitalize on Opioid Addiction Treatment." *Managed Healthcare Executive*, 2 Mar. 2018, modernmedicine.com. Accessed 22 June 2018.

7. Edlin, "Scammers, Fraudsters Capitalize on Opioid Addiction Treatment."

8. "Rehab Success Rates and Statistics." *American Addiction Centers*, n.d., americanaddictioncenters.org. Accessed 22 June 2018.

CHAPTER 8. CRIME, RACE, AND PUNISHMENT

1. Kaitlyn Schallhorn. "What Is MS-13, the Violent Gang Trump Vowed to Target?" *Fox News*, 9 Feb. 2018, foxnews.com. Accessed 22 June 2018.

2. "State of the Union: Trump Addresses Parents of Gang Victims." *CBS*, 30 Jan. 2018, cbsnews.com. Accessed 22 June 2018.

3. "Gangs." *FBI*, n.d., fbi.gov. Accessed 22 June 2018.

4. Sari Horwitz. "Sessions Assigns Dozens More Federal Agents to Combat Illicit Opioid Sales Online." *Washington Post*, 29 Jan. 2018, washingtonpost.com. Accessed 22 June 2018.

5. "Drug Trafficking Organization Dismantled." *FBI*, 8 Feb. 2018, fbi.gov. Accessed 22 June 2018.

6. Beatrice Dupuy. "Black Americans 'Whitewashed' from Opioid Epidemic despite Increases in Drug Deaths, Report Finds." *Newsweek*, 26 Dec. 2017, newsweek.com. Accessed 22 June 2018.

7. "A Brief History of the Drug War." *Drug Policy Alliance*, n.d., drugpolicy.org. Accessed 22 June 2018.

CHAPTER 9. WHAT'S NEXT?

1. Rachel Roubein. "Budget Deal Includes $6 Billion to Fight Opioid Abuse." *TheHill*, 7 Feb. 2018, thehill.com. Accessed 22 June 2018.

2. Julia Lurie. "Senators Just Unveiled a Sweeping New Opioid Bill." *Mother Jones*, 1 Mar. 2018, motherjones.com. Accessed 22 June 2018.

3. Lisa Rapaport. "Prescription Opioids Fail Rigorous New Test for Chronic Pain." *Fox News*, 7 Mar. 2018, foxnews.com. Accessed 22 June 2018.

4. "Opioids No Better Than Tylenol for Chronic Pain, Study Finds." *CBS News*, 6 Mar. 2018, cbsnews.com. Accessed 22 June 2018.

5. Paul Armentano. "New Studies Show that Legal Cannabis Access Reduces Opioid Abuse." *TheHill*, 4 Mar. 2018, thehill.com. Accessed 22 June 2018.

6. "Home." *Advocates for Opioid Recovery*, n.d., opioidrecovery.org. Accessed 22 June 2018.

INDEX

ABOUT THE
AUTHORS

DUCHESS HARRIS, JD, PHD

Professor Harris is the chair of the
American Studies department at Macalester
College and curator of the Duchess Harris
Collection of ABDO books. She is the author
and coauthor of recently released ABDO
books including *Hidden Human Computers:
The Black Women of NASA*, *Black Lives
Matter*, and *Race and Policing*.

Before working with ABDO, she authored several other books on the
topics of race, culture, and American history. She served as an associate
editor for *Litigation News*, the American Bar Association Section of
Litigation's quarterly flagship publication, and was the first editor in chief
of *Law Raza*, an interactive online journal covering race and the law,
published at William Mitchell College of Law. She has earned a PhD in
American Studies from the University of Minnesota and a JD from William
Mitchell College of Law.

JOHN L. HAKALA

John L. Hakala is a freelance writer from Minnesota. Before pursuing
a life of writing, he was a nuclear medicine technologist, and he has
published research in the *Journal of Nuclear Medicine Technology*. He
currently travels with his wife, Heidi. John is the chief contributor for the
blog *Liberty by Choice*.